THE
ALLERGEN-FREE
FAMILY COOKBOOK

THE ALLERGEN-FREE FAMILY COOKBOOK

GLUTEN-FREE, DAIRY-FREE, CASEIN-FREE, SOY-FREE, AND NUT-FREE RECIPES

ERICA DANIELS

FOREWORD BY
KIM STAGLIANO

Skyhorse Publishing

Visit our website at www.skyhorsepublishing.com.

10 9 8 7 6 5 4 3 2 1

Library of Congress Cataloging-in-Publication Data is available on file.

Cover design by Jenny Zemanek
Cover photo credit: Ed Cunicelli
Interior photography by Tom Daniels

Print ISBN: 978-1-5107-5997-8
Ebook ISBN: 978-1-5107-6907-6

Printed in China

This book is dedicated to my daughter, Scarlett Hope.

Hope that autism wouldn't be your fate.

Hope that you will always feel safe and loved.

Hope that I can teach you strength and independence.

Hope that I can give you everything you deserve.

Hope that all of your dreams will come true.

There is not a day that goes by when my heart doesn't break from everything Leo's autism has taken from you. It's not fair and it's okay to feel that way. Except, you don't feel that way. Instead, you are Leo's best friend, teacher, protector, and biggest fan.

You are also *my* teacher. You have taught me about love, acceptance, selflessness, and sacrifice. You connect with your brother's soul in a way no one else can. You see Leo for Leo and not for his disabilities. You love and accept Leo for exactly who he is. You are the most beautiful person I have ever known.

TABLE OF CONTENTS

All Summer Long   111

One Side Is Enough   119

FOREWORD

As an Italian American granddaughter and daughter, "Eat! Eat!" has been part of my vocabulary since I tasted my first tortellini as a toddler. As an autism mother, "WHAT'S IN THAT?!" replaced the love-filled invitation to "Eat!"

Think about food—it's a mother's first gift to her child in her breast milk. It soothes us when we're sick. It makes us smile on our birthday. It signifies holidays. Food is so much more than mere calories and sustenance.

Now imagine having a child with autism for whom foods can mean pain, distress, perseverance, and constant battles. Parents learn early in their autism journey that "the diet" can be a huge part of treatment. But the thought of overhauling much of what you had learned in the kitchen or, for some, having to learn how to cook from scratch is just so daunting that many never get started. And their kids might be losing out on not only an effective treatment but also a chance to create family moments and learn valuable life skills.

Erica has created a cookbook that guides the reader through the process of using food as both medicine and a chance to convey love. The results are sure to be delicious and nutritious, and if they help your child feel better? That's a recipe for success.

Mangia!

Kim Stagliano

All of the recipes in this book are prepared without some of the most common food allergens such as gluten, wheat, dairy, casein, soy, tree nuts, peanuts, fish, shellfish, and sesame. I do use eggs; however, you can substitute them easily with egg substitutes, applesauce, or apple cider vinegar in many of the recipes.

All ingredients I use are organic wherever and whenever possible. All recipes yield family-sized servings in about three to six portions.

This book is not intended to provide medical advice. I am not a doctor, nutritionist, or chef; I am *just* a mom who cooks. The information in this book is based on what I have found helpful for my child and family. Be sure to consult with a dietitian or other medical professionals to know what's exactly right for your child.

Please use caution when cooking with your children. Use your judgment as to what your child's abilities are when handling sharp kitchen utensils, hot ovens, and stovetops. Encourage your child to participate safely and according to their skill level. Always supervise kitchen activities with your child.

INTRODUCTION

What Is Autism?

- Autism spectrum disorder (ASD) and autism are both general terms for a group of complex disorders of brain development. These disorders are characterized, in varying degrees, by difficulties in social interaction, verbal and nonverbal communication, and repetitive behaviors. With the May 2013 publication of the DSM-5 diagnostic manual, all autism disorders were merged into one umbrella diagnosis of ASD. Previously, they were recognized as distinct subtypes, including autistic disorder, childhood disintegrative disorder, pervasive developmental disorder-not otherwise specified (PDD-NOS), and Asperger syndrome.

  Source: https://www.autismspeaks.org/what-autism

- The American Psychiatric Association's *Diagnostic and Statistical Manual of Mental Disorders, Fifth Edition* (DSM-5) provides standardized criteria to help diagnose ASD.

A. Persistent deficits in social communication and social interaction across multiple contexts, as manifested by the following, currently or by history (examples are illustrative, not exhaustive; see text):

1. Deficits in social-emotional reciprocity, ranging, for example, from abnormal social approach and failure of normal back-and-forth conversation; to reduced sharing of interests, emotions, or affect; to failure to initiate or respond to social interactions.

2. Deficits in nonverbal communicative behaviors used for social interaction, ranging, for example, from poorly integrated verbal and nonverbal communication; to abnormalities in eye contact and body language or deficits in understanding and use of gestures; to a total lack of facial expressions and nonverbal communication.

3. Deficits in developing, maintaining, and understand relationships, ranging, for example, from difficulties adjusting behavior to suit various social contexts; to difficulties in sharing imaginative play or in making friends; to absence of interest in peers.

Severity is based on social communication impairments and restricted, repetitive patterns of behavior.

B. Restricted, repetitive patterns of behavior, interests, or activities, as manifested by at least two of the following, currently or by history (examples are illustrative, not exhaustive; see text):

1. Stereotyped or repetitive motor movements, use of objects, or speech (e.g., simple motor stereotypes, lining up toys or flipping objects, echolalia, idiosyncratic phrases).

2. Insistence on sameness, inflexible adherence to routines, or ritualized patterns of verbal or nonverbal behavior (e.g., extreme distress at small changes, difficulties with transitions, rigid thinking patterns, greeting rituals, need to take same route or eat same food every day).

3. Highly restricted, fixated interests that are abnormal in intensity or focus (e.g., strong attachment to or preoccupation with unusual objects, excessively circumscribed or perseverative interests).

4. Hyper- or hyporeactivity to sensory input or unusual interest in sensory aspects of the environment (e.g. apparent indifference to pain/temperature, adverse response to specific sounds or textures, excessive smelling or touching of objects, visual fascination with lights or movement).

Specify current severity:

- Severity is based on social communication impairments and restricted, repetitive patterns of behavior.

- Symptoms must be present in the early developmental period (but may not become fully manifest until social demands exceed limited capacities, or may be masked by learned strategies in later life).

- Symptoms cause clinically significant impairment in social, occupational, or other important areas of current functioning.

- These disturbances are not better explained by intellectual disability (intellectual developmental disorder) or global developmental delay. Intellectual disability and autism spectrum disorder frequently co-occur; to make comorbid diagnoses of autism spectrum disorder and intellectual disability, social communication should be below that expected for general developmental level.

Source: www.cdc.gov/ncbddd/autism/hcp-dsm.html

What Is Cooking?

- "The practice or skill of preparing food by combining, mixing, and heating ingredients."

Source: Oxford Dictionaries, www.oxforddictionaries.com/us/definition/american_english/cooking

What Is Autism to a Mother?

- ♥ Heartbreak
- ♥ Denial and rejection
- ♥ Loss and grief
- ♥ Pain
- ♥ Envy
- ♥ Desperation
- ♥ Massive responsibility
- ♥ Fear
- ♥ Disappointment
- ♥ An epidemic
- ♥ Isolation
- ♥ No friends
- ♥ New friends
- ♥ Post-traumatic stress disorder
- ♥ Depression
- ♥ Broken traditions
- ♥ New traditions
- ♥ Difference
- ♥ Hope
- ♥ Acceptance
- ♥ Special needs
- ♥ Education
- ♥ Doing anything to communicate with your child
- ♥ A smile in your heart every time your child speaks a word, especially "Mommy"
- ♥ Tantrums
- ♥ Obsessive compulsiveness
- ♥ Anxiety
- ♥ Life-threatening food allergies
- ♥ Wondering why
- ♥ Wondering: "Why me?"
- ♥ Wondering: "Why my child?"
- ♥ Why, why, why?
- ♥ Google
- ♥ Mother warriors
- ♥ Passion
- ♥ A full-time 24/7 job
- ♥ Forty to sixty hours a week of therapy
- ♥ Learning a new language
- ♥ ABA, VB, RDI, SPL, IEP, OT, PT
- ♥ "Welcome to Holland"
- ♥ A label
- ♥ Labeled an anti-vaxxer
- ♥ Searching for answers
- ♥ No answers, no cure
- ♥ Biomedical treatments
- ♥ Spending every dollar to try to recover your child
- ♥ Accepting that you can't recover your child
- ♥ Financial ruin
- ♥ Fighting with school districts
- ♥ Fighting with insurance companies
- ♥ Advocacy
- ♥ Hurt siblings
- ♥ Beautiful-hearted siblings
- ♥ Fear of bullies
- ♥ Fear of the future
- ♥ Never taking anything for granted again
- ♥ Perspective
- ♥ Broken-hearted grandparents
- ♥ Judgment from strangers

- ♥ Judgment from family
- ♥ Worrying about abuse
- ♥ Wondering what will happen when I die
- ♥ What keeps me up at night
- ♥ A strange and beautiful journey
- ♥ A medical mystery
- ♥ Becoming a medical detective
- ♥ Constant state of high alert
- ♥ Special diets
- ♥ Food
- ♥ Finding your child's gifts
- ♥ Working ten times as hard to develop those gifts
- ♥ Desperation to connect with your child
- ♥ Acceptance
- ♥ Finding a way in to connection
- ♥ Love
- ♥ Cooking with Leo

What Is Cooking to a Mother?

- ♥ Love
- ♥ Nutrition
- ♥ Tradition
- ♥ Health
- ♥ Family
- ♥ Messes
- ♥ Bonding
- ♥ Holidays
- ♥ Heritage
- ♥ Memories
- ♥ Children
- ♥ Full bellies
- ♥ A labor of love
- ♥ Family meals
- ♥ The kitchen, the heart of the house
- ♥ Making soup for your sick child
- ♥ Making your child's favorite meal when they are having a bad day
- ♥ A responsibility
- ♥ Pushing through even when you are tired or don't feel like it
- ♥ Teaching your children to try new things
- ♥ Better than ordering pizza
- ♥ Necessary
- ♥ An important life skill to pass on to your children
- ♥ Enjoying your children's feelings of accomplishment
- ♥ Encouraging your children to help
- ♥ Knowing it's OK if they sometimes don't want to help and just want to play with their iPads
- ♥ Teaching children to have manners and to clean up after themselves
- ♥ A simple and fun activity to share with your children
- ♥ Bonding, connecting, and spending time with your children

What Is *The Allergen-Free Family Cookbook?*

The Allergen-Free Family Cookbook is not just a cookbook filled with recipes and quick dinners. It is a story of a mother and her child, a story of a mother desperate to connect with her severely autistic son. *The Allergen-Free Family Cookbook* is a gift that came from years of hard work, dedication, persistence, and emotional and physical pain for both Leo and I. Our gift is that we have *finally* connected. Leo and I cook together and share something that we both enjoy. When we cook, we create, laugh, dance, act silly, and, most importantly, spend quality time together. I believe that from every hardship comes a gift, many gifts in fact, and I hope our story inspires you to find your own child's gifts.

This is my story of connecting with Leo through the most essential household activity—cooking. This is our love story.

THE "A" EPIDEMIC

Autism, Asperger's, Allergies, Asthma, ADHD, Autoimmune Disease, Alzheimer's . . .

Why are our children neuro-developmentally disabled and sick? Developmental disabilities are on the rise at staggering rates, and we have to ask ourselves why this is happening. Autism, Asperger's, allergies, asthma, apraxia, ADHD, and autoimmune disease are all variations of

immune dysfunction and neurotoxicity. When you are toxic, you get sick in your body and your brain . . . you get autism or some variation of it.

On March 27, 2014, the Centers for Disease Control and Prevention (CDC) released new data on the prevalence of autism in the United States. This surveillance study identified 1 in 68 children (1 in 42 boys and 1 in 189 girls) as having autism spectrum disorder (ASD).[1]

The Autism Research Institute shared from a study:

The responses from 150 males with autism, aged 6 to 18 years, as well as 135 of their parents, showed that comorbid anxiety and depression were associated with impaired treatment outcomes, poorer quality of life, and increased suicide risk.[2]

---

1. www.cdc.gov

2. "Prevalence, structure and correlates of anxiety-depression in boys with an autism spectrum disorder" Centre for Autism Spectrum Disorders, Bond University, Robina, Queensland 4225, Australia, and Brain-Behaviour Research Group, University of New England, Armidale, New South Wales 2351, Australia,
https://www.researchgate.net/publication/289600597_Prevalence_structure_and_correlates_of_anxiety-depression_in_boys_with_an_autism_spectrum_disorder

The Asthma and Allergy Foundation of America reported in 2012:

- Researchers think nasal allergies affect about 50 million people in the United States.

- Allergies are increasing. They affect as many as 30 percent of adults and 40 percent of children.

- Allergic disease, including asthma, is the fifth leading chronic disease in the U.S. in people of all ages. It is the third most common chronic disease in children under 18 years old.

- Children have food allergies more often than adults. Eight foods cause most food allergy reactions. They are milk, soy, eggs, wheat, peanuts, tree nuts, fish, and shellfish.

- Peanut is the most common allergen. Milk is second. Shellfish is third.

- Researchers think about 6 million children in the U.S. have food allergies. Most of them are young children.

- Also, 38.7 percent of food-allergic children have a history of severe reactions.

- In children with food allergies, 30.4 percent are allergic to multiple foods.

The Centers for Disease Control (CDC) reported in 2011:

- Approximately 11 percent of children 4–17 years of age (6.4 million) have been diagnosed with ADHD as of 2011.

- The percentage of children with an ADHD diagnosis continues to increase, from 7.8 percent in 2003 to 9.5 percent in 2007 and to 11.0 percent in 2011.

- Rates of ADHD diagnosis increased an average of 3 percent per year from 1997 to 2006 and an average of approximately 5 percent per year from 2003 to 2011.

- Boys (13.2 percent) were more likely than girls (5.6 percent) to have ever been diagnosed with ADHD.

Now in 2017, almost five years beyond the last reported data available, we have to wonder what these numbers would look like!

Autism is not a disease but rather a collection of symptoms mostly describing atypical childhood behaviors and development. What textbooks don't describe about autism is the common, consistent, and chronic physical health issues our children experience. Children with autism commonly have comorbid gastrointestinal disease, immune dysfunction, environmental and food allergies, asthma, metabolic disorders, vitamin deficiencies, and seizures. More recent and current research is confirming this pattern.

What are we doing different now and why are our children becoming increasingly sick and neurologically challenged? We *now* agree—parents always knew and scientists are catching on—that autism has an environmental component. But we still cannot agree on *what* that component is.

My answer is quite simple. Through all of mankind's miraculous innovations in agriculture, medicine, and technology, we are changing the course of the human race. We are blinded by our advancements and overlook the effects this is having on our children and future generations to come. There is always a negative to a positive, a pro to a con, and a side effect of a benefit, culminating in a butterfly effect. It seems very obvious if you think logically about it. Mother Earth is suffering the consequences of our wanton use of her. The more we build and the more we use natural resources, the less we have. Global warming, extinction, and pollution are upon us. It only makes sense that we as a human race are affected by the same causes of the earth's deterioration.

We all possess varied genetic predispositions to different diseases and environmental toxins. Why is it that people can live in similar ways in similar areas of the world and be exposed to the same elements, but some get sick and others don't? I think of autism in the same way I think about cancer. Why can one person smoke all of his or her life and never get cancer, while another person suffers the disease even after quitting smoking for ten years? Some children have a genetic predisposition to be affected or insulted by one or more environmental triggers. Our immune systems must have adapted and changed over time by the influences of society's modern advancements. Human and fetal exposure to things such as cellular signals, genetically modified foods, pesticides, germs, toxins, heavy metals, viruses, vaccines, chemicals, medications, power lines, and water and air pollution is largely untested. Common sense tells me that we are slowly seeing the effects of all these things. My conclusion is that we are changing the course of humanity, and we should be very scared.

Again, I am not a scientist, a physician, or an environmental expert; however, I do know that the environment affects our health for a fact. If we are exposing ourselves to and consuming a load of chemicals and toxins (many developed to kill other living creatures, such as insects), there must be a consequence.

"You are what you eat." Isn't that what they say?

Resources

Fortunately, there are many wonderful autism organizations to help and support families affected by autism. Some that you may want to add to your favorites are:

Age of Autism

www.ageofautism.com

Autism at Skyhorse Publishing

www.facebook.com/AutismAtSkyhorse

Autism File

www.autismfile.com

Autism Hope Alliance

www.autismhopealliance.org

Autism Media Channel

www.autismmediachannel.com

Autism One

www.autismone.org

Autism Research Institute (ARI)

www.autism.com

Autism Society of America (ASA)

www.autism-society.org

Autism Speaks

www.autismspeaks.org

Center for Autism and Related Disorders

www.centerforautism.com

Autism Parenting Magazine

www.autismparentingmagazine.com

Doug Flutie, Jr. Foundation for Autism

www.flutiefoundation.org

Elizabeth Birt Center for Autism Law & Advocacy

www.ebcala.org

Epidemic Answers

www.epidemicanswers.org

Fearless Parent

fearlessparent.org

Generation Rescue

www.generationrescue.org

Greater Philadelphia Autism Society

www.asaphilly.org

Green Med Info

www.greenmedinfo.com

Health Choice

www.healthchoice.org

HollyRod Foundation

www.hollyrod.org

Medical Academy of Pediatric Special Needs

www.medmaps.org

Mercola Health News

www.mercola.com

National Autism Association (NAA)

www.nationalautismassociation.org

www.nationalautismny.org

National Vaccine Information Center

www.nvic.org

Talk About Curing Autism (TACA)

www.tacanow.com

Thinking Moms' Revolution

www.thinkingmomsrevolution.com

Weston A. Price Foundation

www.westonaprice.org

Wrights Law

www.wrightslaw.com

"SPECIAL DIETS"

When I think about this I need to take a deep breath.

I sigh because of how overwhelming it has been and still can be. My son, Leo, doesn't just need a "special diet"; he has anaphylactic food allergies that could kill him. Think about that: if a food could kill you, and if you have a child with autism or another disability who doesn't understand this concept or the concept of death. Now, you have to send this child out into the world where something that looks tasty is a threat to their life. The anaphylactic allergy in itself is challenging enough with the complication of the disability. I have images of school lunchrooms being like a minefield for these children. Terrifying.

Having peanut butter in a room with Leo gives me the same feeling as having a loaded gun here. Initially, I was overwhelmed with the fear of having to check labels for peanuts and tree nuts. Life as I knew it was over. Now, I am familiar with almost every allergy-free food brand, where to find it, how to read the labels, and which market sells which allergy-free items like the back of my hand. It took me years to learn all of this without having to carry around reference guides and look up ingredients I wasn't sure of.

After food allergy and gastrointestinal testing, we realized that we needed to remove almost everything from Leo's diet. Leo would show IgE and IgG reactions to so many different foods, and it would change each time we tested it. This testing was the first sign that Leo's immune system was impaired. Leo started out on a nut-free, then gluten-free, then dairy-free diet. From there, we moved into an allergy-elimination diet. I removed all the foods that Leo tested positive to and showed antibodies against. After some time, I slowly added certain foods back into his diet one at a time. This is a true labor of love, my friends. Fortunately, Leo was very young when we tested him and non-verbal at the time. I honestly can't imagine having to do this with an older child. They'll talk back, complain, go on hunger strikes, and complain even more! Surprisingly, Leo focuses a lot on the visuals of the food he eats. For example, he cares about what his food looks like and will eat it if it looks like typical pancakes, waffles, or pizza (though the look of real pizza is much harder to imitate).

The last time Leo ate "real pizza" was in 2007. Pizza is not a healthy choice for anyone, but man, is it good! I still feel guilty that he can't just eat a simple slice of pizza, but I know it will be like a wrecking ball going through his system. I wish he understood this.

I strongly dislike the term "special diet." Leo has severe food allergies, chronic gastrointestinal disease, and a deregulated immune system that can react to any given food at any time. Leo is my little medical mystery that I've tried desperately to solve for many, many years. I have taken Leo to specialists across the country and tried countless interventions and treatments. Leo has been on every "special diet" imaginable (always nut-free, of course). He has been on GFCF diets (gluten-free, casein-free), GFCFSF diets (gluten-free, casein-free, soy-free), SCD (the Specific Carbohydrate Diet), GAPS (the Gut and Psychology Syndrome diet), low-oxalate diets, the Feingold diet, the Body Ecology Diet, and even an Elemental Diet consisting of only liquid nutrition for nine whole months. Oh, Leo hated me for that one! Each diet helped differently in various ways. The Specific Carbohydrate Diet seemed to especially help when Leo was very ill and broke the cycle of stomach pain and constipation. My goal became to create a diet for Leo that was healthy, practical, and not alienating. Eventually this became the goal for the whole family.

The diet I have crafted for Leo and our family came from pulling different things from all these special diets. Today, his diet consists of organic whole foods, wherever possible, and unprocessed non-GMO foods that are free of most common food allergens. I have come to look at our diet not as a "special diet" but simply as a *healthy* diet.

For as long as I can remember, Leo has always had an obsession with food. He will eat as much as I let him eat, and it seems as if he never feels full. He doesn't tell me himself, but that's what I think. I think for him a lot—we are like E. T. and Elliott. Leo is always in and out of the kitchen, opening cabinets, opening the fridge, taking food out, leaving the fridge open, constantly asking for food and snacks, and thinking about his next meal. It has been like this since he was young and it used to drive me crazy! According to other parents, their children who deal with autism also tend to eat like there is no bottom.

We know ASD kids have gastrointestinal issues, and I often wonder whether our kids crave food and eating because of these conditions. Are their bellies hurt and are these cravings a result of their bodies trying to ease the pain? Or, are we as parents part of the problem when we put them on all these special diets and impose dietary restrictions? As warrior moms, we strictly limit our children's diets, sometimes even before seeking medical advice, because we will try anything to make them feel better. We know there is something wrong in severe cases when our children are severely constipated, have chronic diarrhea, and push their bellies against things, and some children with autism have such debilitating gastrointestinal issues that it consumes everything. Whatever it is, I've noticed that our children often improve greatly when they have healed their guts with both medical and dietary treatment. I truly believe in the gut-brain connection, and more and more there is an abundance of research to support this.

Recognizing that your child has a significant GI problem is difficult. Most children with autism aren't able to communicate their pain to us, and it often comes across in aggressive or self-injurious behaviors. Additionally, finding a doctor who believes us when we say our children are suffering in pain is very challenging. I frequently hear stories of medical professionals dismissing children's pain by simply saying that it is all "just part of autism." "Give him more fiber," a gastrointestinal doctor from the Children's Hospital of Philadelphia said to me.

Fortunately, most newly diagnosed families can now find support through groups like Talk About Curing Autism (TACA, www.TACAnow.org) and Generation Rescue. The TACA website is an amazing resource with GFCFSF diet tips, how to get started, and how to manage your budget. TACA will also offer you a parent-mentor who will help you get started on your journey in all areas of autism. TACA is the true meaning of "families helping families," and TACA has been able to develop many very valuable resources to support families affected by autism. Before I knew about TACA, I had learned a lot of this information by traveling the country with Leo to see specialists. When I finally found TACA much later in my journey and started to talk to other members, I felt like saying, "Where have you been?"

Parents often start with gluten- and casein-free diets (as TACA advises). As we read deeper, we begin to become amateur nutritionists. For many years, we worked with a top autism nutritionist in Austin, Texas, keeping food logs, having very expensive appointments, and searching local farmers' markets for things like duck eggs and bison. This was very helpful, but it was also very costly.

Leo showed a very mild positive allergy test result to gluten and dairy on paper. If I hadn't seen it with my own eyes, I wouldn't have believed it. Sometimes after eating gluten, he would transform into a giddy, wild maniac; dairy, on the other hand, caused him to vomit from day one. Corn, however, is the worst for Leo—he becomes a Tasmanian devil after consuming it. Sometimes during summer barbecues I will let him have corn because he absolutely loves it; I just load him up with enzymes and prepare for the worst.

I've noticed that when I eat gluten myself, I feel bloated. It's not just a problem for our kids; it's an issue for a lot of people, young and old. One of my closest girlfriends is actually allergic to casein, but, despite my constant urgings, she refuses to try out gluten- and dairy-free diets, even if just for a week. Another close friend has had severe stomach problems and other health issues for years, and I lecture her frequently about removing gluten and casein from her diet. They haven't listened to me yet. It's hard when you're an adult and you have already cultivated your own eating habits and histories. I strongly suggest trying these diets out for yourself; you may just feel a whole lot better. If you cook and eat by example, you will have a much easier time changing the eating habits of your entire family.

Leo was scoped by a pediatric autism-gastroenterologist in New York when he was two years old. The procedure revealed lesions, inflammation, and chronic gastrointestinal disease. The doctor came to us and said, "Can you start the diet tomorrow?" At that time, the GFCF diet was just becoming popular in the autism community, and it was known as "the diet." I looked down at my huge pregnant belly—oh yeah, I was having a baby in three days—and I looked over at Leo's father. Then I turned to the doctor and said, "Yes!"

You see, we'll do anything at any time to help our children. We are desperate for answers and treatments in order to help our children recover their health. This wonderful physician also gave us some of the most valuable advice I've ever received to this day for our little Scarlett Hope who was about to be born ("Hope" for the *hope* that she wouldn't have autism). Because of Leo's history of food allergies, GI symptoms, and autism, the doctor suggested that Scarlett only have medical hypoallergenic infant formula from day one. He recommended not introducing any foods to Scarlett other than the formula until she was a year old. Scarlett has never had any GI problems. There was no baby reflux, she slept well, she never fussed, and she is allergic to *nothing*. She is the healthiest kid I know! That very afternoon in New York was also the day Leo ate his last "real pizza," the famous New York pizza, coincidentally. That day, our lives and diets changed forever.

During that time, it was very difficult to find a doctor who worked with children who had "behavioral" problems and who could not communicate their pain. Most pediatric GI doctors wrote symptoms like constipation and tantrums off as being "autistic." Now, there are physicians, some at large prominent children's hospitals, who help heal the guts of children with autism and who are also pioneers in that field of research. Dr. Timothy Buie at Boston's Children's is likely the leading expert in autism and gastrointestinal research now, and he's close enough for us to drive to once a year. If you can't access a specialist like this, don't worry. Contact support groups in your area to locate the right medical help. When in doubt, find a TACA mom!

After Leo's heavy GI inflammation was healed through medical treatment and dietary changes, I found that the best consistent remedy for him was to eat a variety of healthy and allergen-free foods, instead of being on a certain "special diet." It is also a healthy way to eat for the entire family, and my own health has improved greatly. Unfortunately, I had to go through a lot to get to this point. I hope our story helps you get there faster. Have faith that your child can and will feel better. If your child's teacher or another parent ever asks if your child is on a "special diet," you can smile and simply say, "My child is on a healthy diet." I find it so strange that others might judge me for not feeding my child chicken nuggets and fries for every meal.

I don't know exactly how or when it all came together—Leo's obsession with food, confirmation of his gastrointestinal disease, my need to control everything he eats, the long winter days I spent trying to entertain him and keep him out of trouble, my desperation to connect with my son, or my family's desire to bond and share meals together—but everything *did* fall into place, and it is the best thing that has happened to our health and our little family. This book is our recipe of love.

Special Diet Acronyms and Definitions

- NF: nut-free diet

- GFCF: gluten-free, casein-free diet

- GFCFSFNF: gluten-free, casein-free, soy-free, nut-free diet

- SCD: Specific Carbohydrate Diet

- GAPS: Gut and Psychology Syndrome diet

- Body Ecology Diet: Focused on restoring "inner ecology" of your body by eating certain foods and food combinations

- Raw diet: Promoting healing through raw foods

- Elimination diet: Eliminating foods that you are allergic or sensitive to

- Rotation diet: Rotating foods to reduce allergic reactions

- Low-oxalate diet: Avoiding and limiting foods with high oxalates

- Paleo diet: Based on the types of foods presumed to have been eaten by early humans, consisting chiefly of meat, fish, vegetables, and fruit and excluding dairy, grain products, and processed food

- Feingold diet: Avoiding food additives to control hyperactivity

- Elemental diet: Liquid diet that contains all the basic nutrients your body needs while giving the bowels a rest

- Ketogenic diet: High-fat, adequate-protein, low-carbohydrate diet that in medicine is used primarily to treat difficult-to-control (refractory) epilepsy in children

Gastrointestinal support for many of these special diets typically includes supplements such as probiotics and digestive enzymes.

Leo's healthy diet: Choosing foods that are non-GMO, whole, organic, and low in grain, with sugar in moderation. Rotating those foods to provide variety, with the overall goal of boosting the immune system and achieving gastrointestinal and whole body health. Allowing Leo to partake in certain foods on special occasions, cheating once in a while, and enjoying food socially—essentially, a healthy diet!

Shopping special diets is so much easier than it used to be, but still hard work. Most stores have online lists for special diets and food allergies now. Here are a few from my favorite stores.

Whole Foods: www.wholefoodsmarket.com/healthy-eating/special-diets

Trader Joe's (you can apply your own filters to search): www.traderjoes.com/home/products/category?categoryId=8

Wegmans: shop.wegmans.com/shop/categories?tags=gluten_free

Healing Our Children's Guts

Children with gut issues, such as yeast/bacteria overgrowth or digestive diseases can develop phenol and salicylate intolerances as a result of leaky gut syndrome. The original "special diet" developed to address behavior and hyperactivity in children was the Feingold diet. My brother was hyperactive as a child and our pediatrician had my mother put him on this diet back in the seventies. Dr. Feingold had discovered through his work that food additives, dyes, and salicylates were causing physical and even behavioral reactions in his patients. Food additives and dyes are manmade chemicals that contain no nutritional value and, in my opinion, should not be intended for human consumption. Conversely, some food phenolic compounds have antioxidant qualities that are helpful in removing toxins and heavy metals from the body. This brings me to my theory that all natural foods from the earth contribute to positive overall health if our guts are healthy. When our guts are not healthy, any food, even the most organic, natural, perfect, and untouched apple from Eve's tree, can disrupt our systems. Maintaining a healthy gut and immune system requires a healthy balance of whole and natural foods. A healthy diet is the best special diet in my opinion.

Having said that, as a mom and the mother of a child with autism, I know it can be very difficult to get your child to eat a variety of foods. Leo would eat grapes for every snack if he could. When we realize we need to change our child's diet, it is usually because our child is already sick and we have to repair the damage. At this stage, more intervention and restrictions need to be made. But have patience, keep cooking, keep offering new foods, and don't give up. Eventually we can get to a place where a variety of healthy, traditional family meals will grace our tables—and our guts.

Some examples of foods that are high in phenols are:

Highest	Moderate	Mild
Raisins	Broccoli	Vanilla w/alcohol
Prunes	Peppers	Chocolate/Cocoa
Strawberries	Cucumber (with skin)	Coffee
Raspberries	Mushrooms	Vinegar
Apricots	Radishes	Pepper
Blackberries	Tomatoes	Cayenne
Blueberries	Zucchini	Cinnamon
Cranberries	Mushrooms	Cumin
Oranges	Okra	Curry
Plums	Watercress	Dill powder
Apples		Honey
Cherries		Horseradish
Grapes		Oregano
Grapefruit		Paprika
Kiwi		Rosemary
		Sage
		Tarragon
		Turmeric
		Thyme
		Worcestershire sauce

A general rule of thumb is that red foods are higher in phenols, so when your child exhibits symptoms, choose green grapes over red, or choose Granny Smith apples over Red Delicious. You get the idea.

Another option is to give your child digestive enzymes to help with difficult foods. Leo is prescribed enzymes as part of his medical treatment plan. There are enzymes that specifically target and help digest phenols. Houston Enzymes makes one called No-Phenol. Houston is a trusted brand and Dr. Houston actively writes and publishes research on the topic.

To Be Organic or Not to Be

I shop organic wherever possible, natural next, and fill in the rest with items containing the least amount of ingredients and additives possible. The idea is to eat as clean as we can. The fewer chemicals you put in your body, the better your health will be. Humans are meant to eat food from the earth and the farm, not from a lab. I know that you can't buy everything organic for various reasons, depending on availability or cost. Just do what you can when you can to consume clean foods.

If you start reading food labels, you will notice that very large quantities of ingredients are listed in mass-produced food products. Many of these ingredients are not even foods; they are additives and preservatives to prolong shelf life or enhance appearance. My general rule is if an item has more than three or four ingredients, I don't buy it. Recently, a lot of progress has been made, and some companies are even volunteering to remove unnecessary ingredients (probably because they have to disclose them if they don't). Consumers are much more savvy than they used to be and the market (no pun intended) is adjusting.

Remember: organic fruits and veggies are labeled beginning with the number 9!

For food allergy parents, we can now skip to the bottom of a food label to find a list of common allergens, thanks to the Food Allergen Labeling and Consumer Protection Act of 2004. This saves a lot of time and adds an extra level of protection for sufferers of food allergies.

Eating clean, natural, and organic can feel intimidating to your budget. Many people don't think it's necessary to spend money on cleaner foods when they can eat something that tastes or looks similar for much less. If you worry about the cost of eating organic and natural, try thinking about it this way: Would you spend the same amount of money on a new pair of sneakers, a yoga class, or a gym membership? Those costs are all investments in your health, right? So why wouldn't you similarly invest in what you actually put into your body? I never understood people who spend their time and money on fitness and who subsequently eat cheap and processed foods. It seems like a paradox.

Parents often talk about "junk food." However, we need to start looking at this concept in a different way: there is no such thing as junk food; there is only junk, and then there is food!

Eating organic is certainly a trend, and some shoppers try to be hip by way of organic talk or labels. However, consumers *are* becoming increasingly educated about food and health choices. If you think it though, eating organic is in fact a return to tradition rather than a trend. Whole foods, organic foods, natural foods, and unprocessed foods are an investment in your health you can't afford not to make.

> "How could we have ever believed that it was a good idea to grow our food with poisons?"
>
> —Jane Goodall

There are many impressive local and national organizations promoting healthy diets for children through education, advocacy, and healthy school lunch initiatives. Here are just a few of my favorites.

- Philly's own world-renowned Chef Marc Vetri is the founder of The Vetri Community Partnership, which promotes healthy bodies and healthy minds through their healthy school lunch initiative and works to empower families to live healthier lives through healthy food and cooking.
  http://www.vetricommunity.org

- Superstar chef and talk show host Rachael Ray founded the Yum-O organization, which focuses on empowering kids and their families to develop healthy relationships surrounding food and cooking.
  http://yum-o.org

- Leo's favorite Food Network show is *Diners, Drive-Ins and Dives*! Host Guy Fieri founded the Cooking with Kids Foundation, dedicated to getting kids in the kitchen as a way of bringing people together. Social skills are difficult for some children with autism, so this is a great initiative.
  www.cwkf.org/

- First Lady Michelle Obama has done wonderful work through her *Let's Move!* initiative, which promotes healthy diet and exercise for young Americans with her "move" to create a healthier generation of American children.
  letsmove.obamawhitehouse.archives.gov/

- A great initiative in food allergy and anaphylaxis awareness is Anaphylaxis: For Reel™. Anaphylaxis: For Reel™ is bringing leading patient and professional advocacy organizations together in their creative approaches to bring attention to anaphylactic allergies.

  "Anaphylaxis: For Reel™ is an effort to bring national attention to the serious and unpredictable nature of anaphylaxis, a life-threatening allergic reaction. The initiative aims to inspire greater understanding about the risks of anaphylaxis through films featuring real-life, everyday stories about the realities of managing potentially life-threatening (severe) allergies."

- Sarah Jessica Parker, Food Allergy Research and Education, Asthma and Allergy Network, FAACT: Food Allergy and Anaphylaxis Connection Team, Kids with Food Allergies (a division of the Asthma and Allergy Foundation of America), and others are working together to help people with severe allergies and their caregivers understand that it's critical to do everything possible to avoid allergic triggers and know how to immediately respond with epinephrine and emergency medical care if anaphylaxis occurs.

COOKING WITH LEO

It's All in the Family . . .

Food is a basic necessity of life. We all need it, we shop for it, we prepare it, and we gather around it. Our social, cultural, and financial situations influence our food choices, but, for the most part, it is our mothers who develop our food habits.

I grew up in a more upper than middle class family on the Main Line just outside of Philadelphia, with a Jewish mother and an Italian father. I am a self-proclaimed "pizza-bagel."

My mother was a stay-at-home mom who took care of my brother and I, the house, and *all* the meals. My mother's house (I give it that name because the rest of us merely lived there amidst her beautiful yet cluttered French Country décor) was neat, clean, and quiet. Her white kitchen was spotless and the pots and pans were always cleaned up before a meal was served. My mother never used recipes, wrote anything down, or measured ingredients with instruments; she would only cook by taste. When you "know" how to cook, this is how it's done. You just feel it.

I never helped my mother cook or clean up. She never asked me to, and I never offered. In fact, she wouldn't let me because then the kitchen wouldn't be cleaned exactly her way. (Mom may have a different recollection!) It wasn't until my Nanny, my Jewish grandmother, the only person who knew the family matzo ball recipe, was dying and I had my own house and children that my mother would begin to grumble that when she passed on, the family recipes would die too. Part of that is a Jewish guilt thing, but the other part scared me because it was totally true. Who would make the rock-hard matzo balls when my Nanny was gone?

My mother's strictest rule was that my brother and I had to be home and at the dinner table at 5:30 p.m. for dinner *every* night. Mom cooked every night and we all sat together and dined. We ate whatever she made, whether we liked it or not, though I can't think of a meal my mother made that I didn't like. Our tastes develop according to what we are fed as children, and what we are used to becomes what we enjoy. This becomes tricky when we need to change our tastes to meet food allergy and dietary restrictions for health reasons. We need to get used to the tastes of more natural, non-processed foods and foods with less sodium and sugar, and we must learn how to appreciate the taste of real whole foods. Whole foods are really all we need to survive; they are much healthier and can be quite enjoyable.

Food made up a large part of my childhood in the everyday meals, special occasions, holiday celebrations, and the time spent as a family. Everything revolved around what we would be eating. There were seven fish courses on Christmas Eve and bagels and lox on Yom Kippur. My mom learned Italian recipes from my father's mother and Jewish recipes from her mother, such as chicken soup and matzo balls. We were culturally rich in food, to say the least!

Today, with differences in lifestyles, an overload of dietary information and speculations, food allergies, and special diets, it seems almost impossible to have one meal together as a family that meets everyone's dietary and taste needs. You have to train your whole family to eat in a certain way, and it won't happen overnight. Kids will be resistant, and husbands perhaps even more so. There will be meals that turn out bad, and that's OK. Don't give up!

Cooking and sharing meals is a family tradition that we don't need to give up simply because a family member has food allergies or autism, or requires a "special diet." In fact, the practice of cooking can become one of the ways you end up connecting with your child.

KITCHEN RULES

1. Be safe, and let your child do as much as safely possible.

2. Get messy.

3. Have fun and act silly.

4. Play with the food . . . appropriately. The whole chicken can do a little dance while you are washing it!

5. Measurements don't have to be exact. Ballpark measurements or substitute ingredients if you need to. We do a lot of shakes, twists, and substitutions in our kitchen.

6. Play music (but not kiddie tunes). Play the music you like and your kids will eventually start grooving along.

7. Drink wine, obviously (parents only, obviously).

8. Let it go, all of it—the worry, stress, and anxiety that goes along with your child's challenges.

9. Use brightly colored pots, mixing bowls, and utensils. Use measuring cups with large numbers printed on them.

10. Take advantage of learning opportunities (whatever stage your child is at). You can learn colors, numbers, and counting in the kitchen.

11. Kiss the cooks a lot.

12. Roll with it and don't stress out if it's not perfect; it won't be!

13. Make clean up a dance party.

14. Cook with love.

Who Has the Time to Measure?

The biggest challenge of writing a cookbook is recording accurate measurements of each ingredient. When Leo and I cook, we don't use exact measurements. We do "shakes," count "pours," or we sing a song to count as mixing time. Sometimes, as with baking, you do have to use exact measurements, and using a large measuring cup with big numbers printed on the side works great.

It's still hard for Leo to control his pouring. Impulse control, fine motor control, and excitement all factor into how Leo cooks. If he really likes something, like sugar or salt, he tends to want to dump it in. To me, it's all good—if too much goes in, we can always balance it out with something else. Cooking is not a science for us; it's a loose, messy, hands-on, touch-and-feel kind of process. When you make these recipes with your children, you will very likely need to make adjustments and corrections if too much of some ingredient goes in!

Cookware

When Leo was diagnosed, we had a six thousand–square foot house and a kitchen to match. It wasn't fancy, but it was big. Unfortunately, autism didn't only bring regression for Leo, it also brought about financial regression, divorce, and two much smaller houses. God, how I miss my old double convection oven. In the old house, I had some Le Creuset equipment, a great big

roasting pan from Williams-Sonoma, and a very large farm table. But this book is about cooking and bonding, and I've learned that apparently you can do that from practically anywhere and with practically anything. I have very few pieces in my current kitchen. A good blender or juicer takes up a lot of space and can be expensive, but it is well worth it. I like colorful pieces also, which helps Leo tell the difference whenever I ask him to grab a certain pot or kitchen utensil.

Nontoxic cookware is a part of cooking healthy. Here are some tips:

- I love glazed cast iron cookware because they can come in fun colors, they heat evenly, and they are sturdy. The downside is that they are heavy and can be high maintenance in the cleaning department. I love Le Creuset, but some popular brands are now coming out with less expensive versions that work similarly.

- Avoid nonstick cookware at all costs. I know, I know. It's easy to use; however, it contains Teflon, which is made from perfluorinated compounds, which are carcinogenic to humans and have been linked to serious health problems. Definitely don't use nonstick if the coating is coming off. I threw mine right in the trash!

- Avoid aluminum pots and pans since aluminum may leach into your food. Aluminum is toxic if ingested and may cause heartburn, headaches, and neurologic and muscular damage. Having said that, I will occasionally use large disposable aluminum pans or trays if I'm making a large batch of something or bringing a dish to someone's house. Sometimes the easy pan is the right choice.

- Ceramic cookware is a safe option as long as there are no chips or cracks. The glazes used in ceramic dishware often contain lead. Cracked or chipping glazes may leach lead into foods.

- Glass bakeware is safer than nonstick. This is what we like to use. Be careful when working with glassware, especially when cooking with kids. Glass mixing bowls are great too; I have an antique set that belonged to my grandmother.

- Stainless steel is a safe option, and it doesn't break. I hardly ever use stainless steel because I get frustrated when food sticks, and it is very hard to clean if you burn something. Nonetheless, it is a safe option.

- If you have a convection oven, you are lucky and I am jealous! Convection will cut down your cooking times by quite a bit. Convection roasting is the best way to roast a chicken or turkey. You'll get moist and crispy chicken, turkey, or vegetables that way.

- Typically, you will not find aluminum foil or plastic wrap in my kitchen (even though my parents are always looking for them to wrap leftover food when they visit). I choose not to use them because I don't need extra metal or plastic around our food. Instead, I use parchment paper or parchment baggies for baked snacks. I use glass containers to store leftovers and a small glass container to pack Leo's lunch. I'm not militant about this stuff though, and I still pack snacks in plastic Ziploc bags and give my children plastic utensils for lunch. We do as much as we can, make gradual changes, and remind ourselves that we don't have to be perfect. Every little bit helps.

Music Makes Life Better

It's a rite of passage for us parents to pass our passions and unique interests on to our children. We dress our kids like mini-mes, impose our favorite sports teams onto them, and nudge them toward theater, science, or art, and even our political beliefs.

It has always been important to me that my kids appreciate *good* music. No, I don't write music or play an instrument, and I especially don't try to sing (except for when I'm in the car and I want to embarrass my daughter at the bus stop). I listen to music . . . all the time. Music has always been my therapy. And when autism entered my life, it created a new playlist, which I have been adding to over time.

Leo has been listening to my music since he was in my belly. He developed an early taste for Pearl Jam, U2, David Gray, Led Zeppelin, and the Black Crowes. I had a secretly proud moment a while back when Leo was with his iPad in the other room and I heard "She Talks to Angels" coming down the hall! When Leo is having a hard time or is overwhelmed with a sensory overload or meltdown, the only thing that

My Music

#hopeforLeo

28 Songs

EDIT

Shuffle

Wonderwall Oasis		4:19	
Fix You Coldplay		4:54	
Not Ready to Make Ni... Dixie Chicks		3:57	
Sweet Pain Blues Traveler		7:41	
Three Little Birds Bob Marley & The Wailers		3:00	
Home American Authors		4:09	
Not Afraid Eminem		4:08	

calms him, most times, is music. I also give quick rock history lessons to Scarlett and quiz her. I'll say, "Who is the lead singer of U2?" and Scarlett would giggle and reply something like, "Bonnie," just to mess with me! Yes, they get our "smart-ass" from us, too! So, make an autism playlist, a cooking playlist, an angry-chic playlist, a work out playlist, a dance party playlist for the kids . . . make lots of playlists!

When you have a child with autism, it can be very difficult to share your passions. My advice is keep doing it; expose your child to the things that are important to you. For us it's cooking and music, though I'm still working on the Syracuse basketball thing!

RECIPE OF LOVE

Ingredients

- ♥ 1 heart full of pure mother's love
- ♥ 1 heap perfectly imperfect little boy
- ♥ 1 cup of hope
- ♥ Dash of perseverance
- ♥ Pinch of acceptance

All recipes in this book yield family-sized servings in about three to six portions.

All ingredients I use are organic wherever and whenever possible.

Directions

- ♥ Love unconditionally
- ♥ Never give up
- ♥ Find your child's gift; it's there
- ♥ Nurture that gift daily
- ♥ Push your child to be the best he or she can be
- ♥ Accept your child's differences
- ♥ Discover that different can be beautiful
- ♥ Wake up every day, and repeat

"The greatest thing you'll ever learn is just to love and be loved in return."
–David Bowie

A Word about Cooking Oils

Discussions about cooking oils have been evolving over the past several years. New information is frequently coming out about what oils to use, which are safe and which are not safe, and why. Initially, I switched to high-heat organic safflower oil, but I have recently read information on some negatives of safflower oils and that it can be inflammatory in some cases.

Many people still use olive oil for cooking, and what they likely do not realize is that at high heats, olive oil becomes carcinogenic. It is okay to use olive oil over low heat to sauté foods or when baking at 350 degrees or lower. Since learning that olive oil becomes carcinogenic at high heats, I now reserve my favorite organic olive oils for dressing cooked vegetables or salads.

One alternative to traditional oils is lard (duck or bacon). It gives your meals a great flavor and lasts a really long time. If you use lard, it is important to make sure the fat is from a clean and high-quality animal source since toxins are usually stored in fat.

Ghee or clarified butter is an option for some; however, it does still contain traces of casein. Ghee is known for its health benefits and stimulations of the digestive system.

Avocado oil is full of healthy fats and a nice oil to cook with or use over cold salads.

More recently, coconut oil has been touted as a wonder oil, for both its cooking and health benefits. However, there is ongoing discussion as to whether coconut is actually a nut or a fruit. When dealing with nut allergies, I err on the side of caution.

Scientifically, when oil is pressed, the properties that cause allergic reactions are no longer present. However, when dealing with life-threatening food allergies, it is unwise and uncomfortable to take any chances. Leo can tolerate coconut oil well, now that his immune system is better.

Palm oil is another option I find useful as a shortening for baking or as a butter substitute. Spectrum makes a butter-flavored palm shortening that is great to bake with.

Food, oils, cooking, and health is an ongoing and evolving scientific discussion. I find that a nice mix and rotation of high-quality organic high-heat cooking oils work for us.

HERE COMES
THE SUN

Early Risers Want to Eat

Kids always seem to wake up early on the weekends but need to be dragged out of bed on school days. What's the deal with that?! Leo usually wakes me up before my alarm goes off at 6:00 a.m., and it's not uncommon for him to rise at 5:30 a.m. I know he will help himself to snacks for breakfast and make a mess of the kitchen. The evidence is always apparent—a trail from the cabinet to the table is likely!

If your child doesn't like to get out of bed, the aroma of breakfast might make it easier, just like coffee works for me. My kids also respond well to music in the morning. You can find cute wake-up songs on the Internet and download them to your phone or their iPad alarm clocks for a happier morning. My mother used to shout, "Good Morning Vietnam!" to wake me up; however, I try to go with something a little less shocking. When Leo was little, I used to sing to the Happy Birthday tune, "Good morning to you, good morning to you, good morning Leo Thomas, good morning to you." I still do this occasionally and he always gets a big smile on his face before he pulls the covers back over his head.

Leo's sister, Scarlett, on the other hand, is a total wild card in the morning. Scarlett is nine going on thirteen. Some mornings, she is up and dressed and ready to go, other mornings I literally have to drag her out of bed whining. Those mornings, we might go through ten different outfits because she "needs" my help, except then everything I pick is bad because I "dress weird," according to her. Her choice of morning tunes consists of the Taylor Swift/ Selena Gomez genre. Oh, and she makes me coffee and eggs on good mornings. She has figured out that mommy needs her coffee start!

Some children, especially those with autism, immunity issues, or metabolic problems, need to eat right away in the morning. Children with more serious issues even need to be woken up during the night to eat in order to keep their metabolic systems regulated. I prefer to have breakfast all together as a family before school, though I go with the flow when the house is rushed and hectic or a child is hungry.

EASY CREAMY COCONUT HONEY YOGURT

The Goods

- ♥ 1 can (13.5 oz) full-fat coconut milk
- ♥ 1 capsule of any probiotic you might be using
- ♥ Organic raw honey
- ♥ Berries (optional)

You'll also need a sterilized glass jar with a lid before you begin.

Some coconut milk brands are now selling coconut milk yogurt in cute, little single servings. These are convenient if you want to send something packaged with your child to school.

Putting Everything Together

1. Pour the coconut milk into the sterilized glass jar.

2. Empty and mix in the probiotic capsule. Put the sealed jar of yogurt in the oven. *Do not turn the oven on.* Close the oven door and turn the oven light on. The closed oven and light should generate a temp of about 105–110 degrees. Leave the jar in the oven for up to 24 hours. The longer you leave it, the more yogurt-y it will become.

3. Place the jar in the fridge to chill until you are ready to serve.

4. Drizzle with organic honey. You can also add berries, or whatever else your child likes. Leo likes to add organic gluten-free Rice Krispies for crunch!

Sometimes, it's nice for our children to have packaged food. It makes them feel more included with the other kids who bring in processed and packaged snacks! However, the premade brands can be very costly, so we use them just for school or to go.

QUINOA PANCAKES, BERRIES ON TOP ONLY

Leo doesn't like it when baked goods, pancakes, or waffles have "things" that are randomly incorporated throughout, like chocolate chips in cookies or berries in muffins. He will pick them out, and there have been times where I've found them strewn around the house. So, it's safer for my floors to put these additional toppings on top of the food so he can push them aside if he's not feelin' it that day.

The Goods

- ♥ 2 cups quinoa flour (allergen/nut-free)
- ♥ 2 tsp baking powder
- ♥ 1½ cups rice milk (vanilla or plain is fine)
- ♥ 2 tsp cooking oil
- ♥ 1 tsp organic vanilla extract
- ♥ 2 free-range organic eggs
- ♥ Non-dairy or vegan butter for the griddle (Earth Balance makes a soy-free butter)
- ♥ 2 tsp organic maple syrup, honey, or agave nectar
- ♥ Berries (optional)

Putting Everything Together

1. In a large bowl, whisk together dry ingredients: quinoa flour, baking powder.

2. In another bowl, whisk together wet ingredients: rice milk, oil, vanilla, and eggs until well combined.

3. Stir the wet ingredients into the dry ingredients and mix until batter is smooth. Let it sit for 5 minutes.

4. Heat large skillet or griddle over medium heat. Melt a bit of the vegan butter so that your pancakes won't stick. You don't need a lot.

5. Pour the batter into the skillet or griddle in ¼ cup scoops, and cook until small bubbles just begin to form on the pancake's surface. Flip.

6. Top with organic maple syrup, honey, or agave nectar. You can also add berries! If you are trying to cut down on sugar, just serve them plain. Leo actually won't use syrup.

I always make extra pancakes, waffles, and sausage. I will often double the recipe and put leftovers in the freezer so I can grab some and put them in the toaster for breakfast before school. Try making this a Sunday morning activity with the family. Making larger batches may take a while, but it's well worth the effort when you're rushing to get everyone out of the house during the week.

"GOOD MORNING, LEO THOMAS" FRUIT SALAD

I always try to serve fruit with breakfast. Some kids are not super hungry in the morning; Scarlett never is. When my kids eat fruit in the morning, I feel better. Most times, Leo will just eat sausage and fruit for breakfast, which is a great low-carb breakfast if you are trying to cut down on sugars or control yeast intake.

The Goods

- ♥ 1 organic banana
- ♥ 1 clementine
- ♥ Handful of organic green grapes
- ♥ Any kind of melon, sliced

You can use any kind of fruit your children like or whatever is in season. The point is that they are eating fruit.

Pack any leftover fruits as a healthy snack at school. You can squirt lemon juice on fruit to keep them from turning brown.

Putting Everything Together

1. Chop the fruit.

2. Arrange on a plate and make it look pretty, or serve as a side to any breakfast item.

I always have fruit in the house. I like to keep a big bowl of seasonal fruit out on the counter in the kitchen. When any of my kids say they are hungry, I point to the bowl for snacks. Keeping nutritious and beautiful fruits out in the kitchen contributes to eating and snacking healthily.

TEFF TOUGH HONEY WAFFLES

The Goods

- ♥ 2 cups organic teff flour (allergen/nut-free)
- ♥ 2 tsp baking powder
- ♥ ½ tsp ground organic cinnamon
- ♥ ¼ tsp sea salt
- ♥ 2 organic free-range eggs, beaten
- ♥ 3 tbsp organic honey
- ♥ 3 tbsp coconut oil or non-dairy butter (we like soy-free Earth Balance)
- ♥ 2 cups organic coconut milk (rice milk is fine too)
- ♥ Organic maple syrup, to drizzle
- ♥ Bananas or any fruit you prefer (optional)

> Trader Joe's carries a nice variety of good quality organic maple syrups.

Putting Everything Together

1. Sift the flour, baking powder, cinnamon, and sea salt into a mixing bowl. With a few quick strokes, stir in the eggs, honey, coconut oil, and coconut milk.

2. Spray your waffle iron with organic coconut oil or other high-heat oil occasionally to keep the waffles from sticking. The texture of teff is different—thick and heavy and it browns and crisps easily—so you will have to get used to working with it.

3. Pour the mixture into a heated waffle iron and cook for 3 to 5 minutes, or until the timer on your waffle iron goes off (if you have one).

4. Set aside on a rack to cool before serving.

5. Top with organic maple syrup, and bananas or any other fruit you prefer.

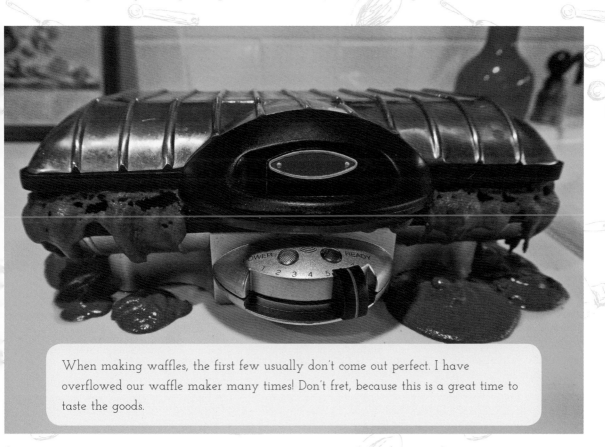

When making waffles, the first few usually don't come out perfect. I have overflowed our waffle maker many times! Don't fret, because this is a great time to taste the goods.

CHICKEN AND APPLE SAUSAGE PATTIES, ROUND ONLY

For years, Leo ate link-shaped breakfast sausages. Then, one day, he only wanted round patties. You pick your battles, if you know what I'm sayin'.

The Goods

- ♥ 2 tbsp organic cooking oil
- ♥ 1 small organic onion, finely chopped
- ♥ 2 organic Granny Smith apples, peeled and chopped
- ♥ ½ cup sage leaves, finely shredded (if your child doesn't like to see green leaves in their food, shred them finely or just leave them out)
- ♥ 1 tsp organic raw honey
- ♥ ½ tsp organic fine sea salt
- ♥ ½ tsp organic ground black pepper
- ♥ ½ tsp organic ground white pepper
- ♥ 1 lb organic chicken

Putting Everything Together

1. Preheat oven to 350 degrees.

2. Heat oil in a large frying pan over medium heat.

3. Add onion, apples, sage, raw honey, sea salt, black pepper, and white pepper into a food processor and pulse. If you don't have a food processor, chop the ingredients finely and mix together.

4. Add the onion-apple-sage mixture to the pan and stir frequently to brown, about 5 minutes. Set aside and let cool.

5. Combine ground chicken and the apple-onion-sage mixture in a mixing bowl and combine thoroughly with your hands, like you would a meatloaf. My kids love to help out with this part (though some kids may not like the feeling). Make sure they wash their hands immediately after touching raw meat.

6. Form 1½-inch round, flat patties.

7. Add a little more oil to the pan and brown patties, about 2 minutes on each side.

8. Transfer patties to a baking sheet and bake in the oven until cooked through, about 10 minutes.

These patties are a great breakfast item, especially if your child is on a low-carb diet. You can serve this with some fruit or eggs for a larger meal. When Leo was on the Specific Carbohydrate Diet, he ate this every morning with fruit.

SCARLETT'S EZ-CHEEZY DAIRY-FREE EGGS

The Goods

- ♥ 1 tsp organic high-heat cooking oil or dairy- or soy-free butter for the pan
- ♥ 2 organic free-range eggs
- ♥ ½ tsp organic fine sea salt
- ♥ ½ tsp organic ground black pepper
- ♥ ¼ tsp organic baking powder
- ♥ ½ cup dairy-free cheese, shredded

Putting Everything Together

1. Heat oil in a frying pan on medium-to-low heat.

2. Wisk eggs, salt, pepper, and baking powder together in a glass bowl.

3. Pour eggs into the pan over medium heat. Sprinkle in shredded cheese.

4. Mix with spatula and don't overcook—fluffy is good!

Shhh . . . I'll tell you a Philly Girl secret. I once had scrambled eggs at a funky little South Philly brunch place that were incredibly fluffy, so fluffy until I had to ask what their secret was. Alas, it was baking powder!

★ COMMONWEALTH of ★
PHILADELPHIA
Founded 1682
"City of Brotherly Love"
PHILADELPHIA MANETO
Let brotherly love endure
Philly
The CITY THAT LOVES YOU BACK
CRADLE of LIBERTY
The QUAKER CITY
The BIRTHPLACE of AMERICA
The CITY of NEIGHBORHOODS
COMMONWEALTH of PENNSYLVANIA

PROBIOTIC BREAKFAST SMOOTHIES

The Goods

- ♥ 2 cups organic mixed fruits or frozen fruit, whatever you prefer
- ♥ 1 cup organic coconut water or organic coconut milk
- ♥ Splash of orange or pineapple juice (optional; Leo doesn't like this!)
- ♥ 1–2 probiotic capsules (Kirkman Labs makes a good line of clean probiotics)

Putting Everything Together

1. Dump the frozen fruit into a large blender.

2. Measure and pour coconut water or milk and juice (optional) into the blender.

3. Start blending on a lower speed, then switch to high until the mixture is smooth. Times will vary depending on what kind of blender you have.

4. Add the probiotics and blend to mix.

Yes, it's that simple. Kids love to feel, watch, and feel the blender.

Be careful when working with blenders as they have sharp parts. Let your kids turn the dial to speed up the blender, and teach them to move it slowly.

Substitute the coconut water or milk with your favorite dairy-free yogurt or ice cream for a special, creamy treat.

HOT FARE

Food is Love

Food is a way through which many friends and family members show us love. People are known for the particular dishes they make, and we connect certain foods to certain people in our lives. We are fed chicken soup when we are sick, we receive special desserts on our birthdays, and we can't wait when Grandma's signature holiday dish makes its yearly appearance.

It can become difficult for members of the family who want to share their love through certain dishes when a child with food allergies and dietary restrictions can't eat all the food on the table. It creates stress for mommas who want our children to be happy and healthy. They already experience difficulty being included with the rest of the crowd due to challenges associated with autism. The best scenario we can hope for is to teach our loved ones about our child's food restrictions and show them ways to "adjust" their dishes so they can still share that love language with our child and make a connection.

When Leo used to see his mom-mom, he would immediately ask for pot roast, which he associated with her. With his limited language and interests, her pot roast was the means through which he could connect with her.

Different people mean different "things" to Leo. Aunt Jackie means Thanksgiving and the tree swing at her house that he loves. Aunt Michelle means fruits and grapes in the fridge, as well as her basement with all those toys. Grandma means pineapple spoon bread and lots of kisses. I'm fairly certain that Leo thinks in pictures, foods, and experiences. With his limited communication skills, Leo sometimes tells me what he wants by naming a favorite dish.

"MOM-MOM" MEANS POT ROAST

I never made a pot roast until my mother-in-law showed me how. My own mother never cooked pot roast. Leo loves his mom-mom, and he loves pot roast! It's always nice when you can make a one-dish meal and feel as if you've covered all the nutritional food bases.

The Goods

- ♥ 3 tbsp organic high-heat cooking oil
- ♥ 4–5 lb organic or natural chuck roast (it makes a big difference using quality, organic meat; try to pick one that doesn't have too much marbling)
- ♥ 1–2 tsp coarse kosher salt (to tenderize the meat)
- ♥ 4 twists cracked organic rainbow peppercorns
- ♥ 1 tbsp organic pressed garlic
- ♥ 2 large organic sweet onions
- ♥ 1 bag organic rainbow heirloom carrots
- ♥ 4–6 stalks organic celery
- ♥ Purple potatoes or any other root vegetables you prefer (purple potatoes have good antioxidant properties)
- ♥ 1–2 cups filtered water, organic beef stock, or leftover bone broth

Putting Everything Together

1. Heat oil over medium heat in a Dutch oven on the stove.

2. Cover the roast evenly on all sides with kosher salt, pepper, and garlic.

3. Peel and cut all vegetables into large, chunky pieces.

4. Brown the roast by searing on all sides over medium-high heat.

5. Place veggies in the pot under and around the roast.

6. Pour the water or stock over the meat and veggies so that about half of the roast is submerged in the liquid. Check the pot occasionally and add more liquid if needed.

7. Cover, turn heat down to low, and cook for 2 to 3 hours.

8. Remove the roast and let sit on a cutting board for at least 5 minutes to cool. Slice meat against the grain.

If you want to include a starch in addition to the potatoes, serve with your favorite gluten-free breadsticks. You don't have to serve just "meat and potatoes" to have a well-balanced meal; and the veggies in this dish are plenty enough for a side.

Mom-mom says that you can't overcook pot roast. Depending on the size of your roast, it may be cooked after about an hour and a half; but the longer and slower it cooks, the softer the meat will become.

THRIFTY, TASTY TURKEY THIGHS

We always play music whenever we cook. Choose songs that match well with the dish or ingredients. For this recipe, I can't help but think of Simon and Garfunkel. Leo loves Simon and Garfunkel; he's listened to them since he was very young. Mellow music calms Leo, especially when he is upset or even in the middle of a meltdown. Give music a try—it makes life better!

The Goods

- ♥ 4 large organic or natural turkey thighs
- ♥ High-heat cooking oil, for the pan
- ♥ Mirepoix:

     1 large organic onion

     2–3 organic celery stalks

     3–4 organic carrots, washed and peeled

     (Traditionally two parts onion: one part carrot: one part celery)
- ♥ 2 tbsp dairy/soy-free butter, melted (I like Earth Balance's soy-free butter sticks)
- ♥ Dry brine seasoning mix:

     1 tbsp kosher salt

     ½ tsp citrus salt

     1 tsp aluminum- and gluten-free baking powder

     ¼ tsp dried organic parsley

     ¼ tsp dried organic sage

     ¼ tsp dried organic rosemary

     ½ tsp dried organic thyme

I love mirepoix. I love saying the word (pronounced "meer-pwah"), I love making it, and I love that you can put it into almost any meat or poultry dish to add flavor and color. The dicing is the tricky part—I do not recommend having your children do any dicing. During the fall season, you can typically find pre-made mirepoix mixes in the produce section. This can save a lot of time! Mirepoix is a great way to squeeze some veggies into your meals, too.

Putting Everything Together

1. Let the turkey thighs sit out for about 30 minutes before cooking.

2. Preheat the oven to 400 degrees. In the meantime, prepare the mirepoix. Evenly and finely dice the onion, celery, and carrot.

3. Heat oil in a frying pan and sauté the vegetables until browned. Place the mirepoix on the bottom of the roasting pan before the turkey goes in.

4. Wash and dry the turkey thighs thoroughly. Place on a roasting rack (if you have one). Use a pastry brush to spread the melted dairy-free butter over the turkey thighs. Kids love doing this; it's like food art. Save a little butter to drizzle on later.

5. Combine salt, baking powder, and herbs to make the dry brine mix.

6. Season thighs with your dry brine mix. Be sure to get some under the skin. Drizzle the remaining butter on top.

7. Cook for 20 minutes at 400 degrees, then lower to 325 degrees and cook an additional 2 to 2½ hours. The inner temperature of the bird should be 165 degrees.

8. Every 30 minutes or so, baste or spoon pan juices over the turkey.

Turkey thighs are the best bang for your buck. They are big, tasty, and very reasonably priced. However, they are a rare sight in the poultry section, so grab them when you see them!

BUDDHA BOWLZ

I like the vibe of this dish. A traditional Buddha bowl or hippie bowl is a bowl resembling the belly of a Buddha that is filled with highly nutritious foods. We add brown rice or quinoa, raw or roasted veggies, and sometimes some leftover chicken for protein.

I let the kids choose how they want to make their Buddha bowls. It's fun for them to have total control of their food sometimes. And, of course, use cute bowls to put the food in.

I am not religious, but if I had to choose I would say that I most relate to the Buddhist philosophy. When you have a child with special needs or any chronic stressor in your life, you need to find a way to feel peaceful. I keep Buddha statues around my house; they remind me to breathe and I try to feel intentionally peaceful. I have one across from my bed; it's the first thing I see when I wake up. Instead of waking up filled with the anxiety of everything I need to accomplish that day, I look at the statue and am reminded to breathe. Practicing yoga and meditation reduces stress and anxiety for adults and children. Leo practices yoga every morning at school.

The Goods

♥ Steamed organic brown rice or quinoa (we like Trader Joe's brand of jasmine rice)

♥ Steamed broccoli and carrots

♥ Leftover grilled chicken (optional)

Putting Everything Together

• Let the kids put whatever they want in their Buddha bowl. Let them own it and gobble it up!

The kids and I sometimes do yoga together. Yoga Pop Ups, a pop-instrumental music group, has a great tribute to Pearl Jam that we like. We line up in front of the fireplace and Scarlett leads. Practice a little yoga and then have a Buddha bowl for dinner instead of pizza night!

NOT-SO-FANCY LEMON TARRAGON CHICKEN

Tarragon was one of my mom's staple flavors. In the summer, we put lemon tarragon chicken on the grill—yum! She would make this dish with cut-up chicken pieces, though you can prepare your chicken in any way—whole, cut-up, or boneless thighs—as long as you get that flavor.

I suspect most parents don't use tarragon when cooking for kids; it does have a kind of licorice flavor to it, but it can also be light and delicious. This recipe is a great instance of traditional styles and flavors being passed down from one generation to the next in my family. While my mother used tarragon for its flavor, what she didn't realize was that it also has many health benefits. I love this dish because I can carry its tradition and be confident that it's also providing nutrition to my children.

The Goods

- ♥ Whole organic chicken, about 3–4 lb bird (or whatever size works for your family), washed and dried
- ♥ 4 tbsp organic high-heat cooking oil
- ♥ 4 organic lemons (I like Meyer when I can find them)
- ♥ 2 tbsp kosher salt
- ♥ 4 twists citrus salt on each side
- ♥ 1 tsp garlic salt (I use garlic salt in everything, and so does my mother)
- ♥ 3 cracks lemon pepper
- ♥ 4 tbsp organic French tarragon (or enough to cover the bird)
- ♥ 1 tbsp organic Herbes de Provence, to sprinkle

French tarragon is also known as "dragon's-wart," so if your child is into dragons, you can have fun talking about a "licorice-tasting dragon's-wort spice to ward off evil monsters."

Putting Everything Together

1. Preheat the oven to 450 degrees.

2. Place the chicken in a roasting pan. Rub oil all over the chicken and save a drop for the end. Let the kids use their hands; it will spread better and it's a sensory delight for them. Have them wash their hands right after.

3. Slice the lemons in half and squeeze two on each side of the chicken. Again, massage the lemon and oil into the chicken. Any leftover lemon can be used to kill bacteria left on your hands or bacteria in the sink.

4. Sprinkle and grind the salts and pepper evenly over the chicken. We practice counting when we grind the salt and pepper. You may have to place your hand over your child's hand to spread evenly. Grinding spices is a good exercise for fine motor strength and control.

5. Cover the chicken with tarragon, spreading generously. This will make the flavor of the dish.

6. Sprinkle the Herbes de Provence last.

7. Drizzle the remaining bit of oil over the bird.

8. Fill the pan about half full with water. This will start your juices.

9. Cook at 450 degrees for 15 minutes. Reduce to 350 degrees, roasting the chicken for 20 minutes per pound. If the wings or legs start to get too crispy or dark, you can cover the tips with a bit of foil.

10. Remove the chicken and let sit for about 10 minutes before slicing and serving. I like to return the cut-up chicken to the pan with the gravy so it absorbs the juices. Once it's sliced, pour the gravy over the top.

I like to serve this with jasmine rice and broccoli. You can also add mirepoix to the roasting pan in step 2 to flavor this dish.

French tarragon has antioxidant properties and is often used as an appetite stimulant. We talk a lot about oxidative stress when we talk about autism and other chronic health conditions. Proper methylation is critical to thinking, fighting infections, and ridding your body of toxins. Some children take MB12 injections to help with significant oxidative stress problems, and adding a little French tarragon to your child's diet is a simple and natural way to add antioxidant support. All around, French tarragon is a rock star of spices for its flavor and health benefits. Use it abundantly!

SCARLETT'S FAVORITE PAPRIKA CHICKEN

The Goods

- ♥ 3 lb boneless skinless organic chicken thighs (or a family-sized package)
- ♥ Organic high-heat cooking oil, to drizzle
- ♥ Kosher salt
- ♥ Organic garlic salt
- ♥ Organic black pepper
- ♥ Organic paprika
- ♥ Organic dark honey

You can use honey from a jar, but it's definitely more fun squeezing it out from a honey bear bottle.

Putting Everything Together

1. Preheat the oven to 350 degrees.

2. Wash and dry the chicken thighs. Line them single file in a glass or ceramic baking dish.

3. Drizzle oil over the chicken.

4. Sprinkle kosher salt, garlic salt, and pepper over the chicken on both sides. Cover the chicken in paprika.

5. Drizzle honey across each piece of chicken two or three times.

6. Mix until the thighs are wet and evenly coated.

7. Cook the thighs for about 40 minutes, occasionally spooning the juices over the chicken.

GRANDMA'S BEEF STEW

The Goods

- ♥ 3 tbsp high-heat organic cooking oil
- ♥ ½ medium organic sweet onion, sliced
- ♥ 3 lb organic grass-fed stew meat, cubed
- ♥ 2 tsp coarse kosher salt
- ♥ 1 tsp organic cracked black pepper
- ♥ Organic dried basil (lots and lots, again we're going to eyeball it)
- ♥ 1 tsp organic garlic salt
- ♥ Pinch organic paprika
- ♥ 1 can organic tomato sauce
- ♥ 1 can organic tomato paste
- ♥ 1 tbsp organic dark brown sugar (I like it sweet so I add a little more)
- ♥ 4–6 rainbow/heirloom carrots, peeled and sliced
- ♥ 4–6 purple and/or yellow potatoes, peeled and sliced (optional, or whatever veggies you prefer)
- ♥ ½ bag frozen mini pearl onions, sliced
- ♥ ½ bag organic frozen French green beans

My kids love to peel carrots, but if I don't supervise Leo the carrots will be pencil thin. He loves it too much! The veggies should be chunky and colorful. If you want a low-starch stew, leave out the potatoes. Leo dislikes potatoes, except for French fries, so I don't always put them in.

Putting Everything Together

1. Heat the oil over medium heat in a large soup or stew pot.

2. Add the onion slices to brown.

3. Add in the meat, and season with salt and pepper. Brown the meat on all sides by stirring frequently.

4. Add in enough basil so that all of the meat is covered on both sides. Add in garlic salt and paprika.

5. Stir in the can of tomato sauce and tomato paste. Add brown sugar. Fill the pot with water until the meat is completely covered with the liquid mixture.

6. Turn down the heat to low and simmer for about an hour, stirring occasionally.

7. Add chopped carrots and potatoes to the pot, cooking for 30 minutes.

8. Add in frozen veggies—the pearl onions and green beans. Simmer on low for another 30 minutes and don't overcook because you want the veggies to be bright and colorful.

You can always add in gluten-free dumplings to make this a truly comforting dish, since everyone loves dumplings. Gluten-Free Dumplings (p. 78) can be prepared alongside the stew and added in after step 8.

GLUTEN-FREE DUMPLINGS

The Goods

- ♥ 2 tbsp cooking oil
- ♥ ½ cup rice milk
- ♥ 1 cup gluten- and nut-free biscuit or baking mix

Putting Everything Together

1. Mix the oil and rice milk together.

2. In a mixing bowl, combine the liquid and biscuit mix.

3. If you're cooking the dumplings in Grandma's Beef Stew (p. 76), raise heat under the stew back up to a soft boil. You can also cook the dumplings in water.

> Comfort food alert! Dumplings make any dish yummier. I love this dish mostly because I get to use my giant red Le Creuset soup pot.

4. Drop a tablespoon of the mix into your stew or water.

5. Lower the stew or water back to a simmer and cover for about 15 minutes.

6. The dumplings should rise to the top when they are cooked.

FOOTBALL SUNDAY TURKEY CHILI

I try to include as many "typical" things as possible in Leo's routine. Sunday is for football, right? So, we put on the NFL games and cook. Leo's isn't really into sports, but sometimes I catch him watching the game, especially when Grandpa is yelling at the TV!

We watch football while we are waiting for the chili to cook. We usually eat chili with GFCFSFNF (gluten-free, casein-free, soy-free, and nut-free) pumpkin muffins. You can buy a good gluten-free muffin mix if you don't feel like baking it from scratch.

The Goods

- ♥ 3 tbsp organic high-heat cooking oil
- ♥ 1 medium sweet organic onion, chopped
- ♥ Whatever veggies you like, fresh or frozen, chopped
- ♥ 2 lb ground turkey (dark meat is much tastier than white meat)
- ♥ 1 tbsp organic chili powder, to taste
- ♥ 1 tsp organic chipotle cayenne pepper, to taste
- ♥ 1 tsp organic garlic salt

- ♥ 1 tsp organic paprika
- ♥ 1 tsp organic ground cinnamon
- ♥ 3 twists of organic cracked rainbow peppercorns
- ♥ 1 tbsp organic ground turmeric
- ♥ 3 tbsp organic dark brown sugar
- ♥ 1 can organic tomato sauce
- ♥ 1 can fire-roasted tomatoes (Trader Joe's has a great one)
- ♥ 1 bay leaf (optional)

I like to use multicolored carrots for pizzazz, mini pearl onions because Leo loves them, and peppers or mushrooms. If your child won't eat big veggies, blend them in your food processor and add them in discreetly.

Turmeric is known to improve immunity and aid in digestion, inflammation, insomnia, respiratory disorders, asthma, bronchitis, and even the common cold. If your child is experiencing bad reflux, this dish may not be suitable. Leo is okay with it now, but he does take an antacid. That's how they advertise antacids on TV anyway, with chili and Mexican foods!

Putting Everything Together

1. Heat the oil and cook the chopped onion in a heavy pot over medium heat, stirring occasionally, until golden. Push the onion to the side of the pot.

2. If you are using fresh vegetables, brown them in the oil but don't fully cook. If using frozen veggies, you will be adding them later.

3. Add the ground turkey. Don't break it up yet; try to keep it in the shape of the package and let it brown on each side. This way, your chili will be chunkier.

4. Add all of the spices and brown sugar (except the bay leaf), while slightly breaking up the turkey.

5. Spread the tomato sauce to cover the meat.

6. Stir the fire-roasted tomatoes into the tomato sauce.

7. Add the bay leaf and stir well.

8. Turn the heat down to low or a simmer and cook uncovered for about an hour.

9. If you are using frozen veggies, add them now.

10. Cook for another 15 to 20 minutes on low heat or until the veggies are cooked but not mushy.

I don't use any beans in our chili because of Leo's peanut allergy. Peanuts are actually a legume, so I personally don't want to take a chance. However, I don't think you are automatically allergic to beans if you are allergic to peanuts. Check with your allergist to learn more about legumes.

Anaphylaxis Is No Joke

Having peanuts near a child who has a severe allergy is like having a loaded gun in reach. Both things can kill. Add in the variable of a child with autism who doesn't understand the concept that a certain food can kill him, and you now have a bomb waiting to go off.

I can write and cook all of the allergy-free recipes I want, but there *will* be times in life when peanuts will just be around. There was a time when food couldn't go near Leo's mouth unless it had passed through my hands first. No matter how careful I am, I cannot control everything. I'm still working on that!

Once, I had *just* been reading about a new study about a possible treatment for peanut allergies when I got a 911 text. 911 text equals "peanut" to me. I ran out the door. I am typically calm under pressure; it's an autism mom thing. When I reached Leo, he appeared to be okay. I gave him Benadryl and sped off to the ER. I was even pulled over on the way to the hospital, which then quickly turned into a police escort. Leo began to go into anaphylaxis slowly, which is not common. It was the same way he had reacted to his initial peanut incident nine years ago. In hindsight, almost nine years without a scare was a blessing. It wasn't until an hour or more after Leo had ingested the peanut product that he started to have trouble breathing and developed hives all over his body. This was *after* he had already received Benadryl and a steroid shot.

I carry a big yellow EpiPen injector with me wherever we go. It is still intimidating even though I have handled various medical treatments with Leo over the years. That day, I had been afraid to give him the EpiPen, which I regretted. The next time, I will give him the EpiPen *right away.*

Thankfully, other than a smashed iPad screen, Leo was okay. The scariest part of the process is that when Leo returns to his routine, he is out of the house and out of my control again. *Breathe*, I say to myself. I say that a lot!

Leo's school *is* currently nut-free; however, it took serious educating and multiple meetings, as it had at his previous schools, to accomplish this. Parents need to educate, advocate, and not back down.

I am not afraid to repeat, once again, to *anyone* who quibbles or tells me that their children will only eat PB&J: "Having peanuts near a child with a severe allergy is like having a loaded gun in reach." I mean, who doesn't love PB&J? It's not personal! For some, peanuts are a matter of life and death. Have a turkey sandwich next time!

BAKED CHICKEN CUTLETS

My daughter does not have food allergies and her diet is not specifically gluten- or dairy-free. She will frequently say things like, "Are those Leo's breadcrumbs?" or, "I don't want Leo's pasta."

In an effort to cook one meal for everyone, I have given up making two different meals for each child. There is no health concern in feeding Scarlett the same diet I feed Leo; in fact, she eats healthier because of Leo. I try not to make a big deal about separating special "diet food" with more typical American choices in my house. The answer I give her is something like this: "Mommy made a dinner that is healthy for all of us, and it tastes really good. Try it." If she continues to complain or doesn't want to eat something that is "Leo's," she can make herself a sandwich or a bowl of cereal. I will not cook another meal, and she usually likes my food anyway. If you have children who can tolerate more typical diets, but you prefer to cook a single meal for everyone, I recommend being firm but encouraging.

The Goods

- ♥ 1 lb organic boneless chicken breasts, washed and dried
- ♥ 2 organic free-range eggs
- ♥ 1 tsp organic sea salt
- ♥ 1 tsp organic black pepper
- ♥ 2 cups Italian-style gluten-free breadcrumbs (see recipe on p. 106)
- ♥ Organic olive oil, to drizzle

You can also use chicken tenderloins to create chicken strips. I sometimes make this for brunch and freeze them for easy weekend lunches.

Note: I usually don't use olive oil whenever I cook at high heats because it can become carcinogenic. However, something about Italian chicken cutlets just doesn't work with any other oil.

Putting Everything Together

1. Preheat the oven to 350 degrees.

2. Cut the larger pieces of the chicken in half.

3. Beat eggs and add salt and pepper. Leo's favorite part is cracking eggs. He does a great job, but will keep adding eggs if I don't limit him!

4. Pour the gluten-free breadcrumbs into a large plastic baggie.

5. Dip the chicken in the egg one or two pieces at a time.

6. Place chicken pieces in the bag with breadcrumbs. This can all be done with a fork if you don't want your child to handle raw chicken and egg. A fork is also helpful for children with fine motor skills.

7. Leave some air in the bag and seal it. Twist until taut, then shake. We sing and dance while we shake—Shake . . . shake . . . shake . . . shake your booooty! The chicken should be fully covered by the end of the booty-shake tune.

8. Drizzle a little bit of olive oil on the bottom of a glass baking dish to prevent the chicken from sticking. Place breaded cutlets in a single layer on the baking sheet.

9. Drizzle more olive oil on top to keep the chicken moist.

10. Bake at 350 degrees for about 40 minutes. You don't have to turn the chicken over. Sometimes I turn the broil on at the end for a minute to crisp the crumbs more.

Serve with organic applesauce and broccoli to make it healthy and simple. My mom used to serve her chicken cutlets with Carlino's ravioli, her homemade sauce, and broccoli. That was a favorite meal of ours growing up, but of course raviolis are *loaded* with gluten and casein, not to mention extremely fattening!

MEATLOAF AND SNEAKY VEGGIES

The Goods

♥   2 organic free-range eggs
♥   ½ cup organic baby carrots, chopped
♥   ½ cup organic green beans, chopped
♥   ½ organic sweet onion, chopped
♥   2 lbs ground organic grass-fed beef
♥   ½ cup Italian-Style Gluten-Free Breadcrumbs (see recipe on p. 107)
♥   1 can organic tomato paste

You can freeze leftover meatloaves for another meal.

If you can't find organic ground meat, go for natural or grass-fed.

Ian's makes good Italian-style gluten-free breadcrumbs if you don't have time to make them from scratch. You can find many gluten-free options at most grocery stores. Just be sure to check the ingredients for other allergens besides wheat.

Putting Everything Together

1.   Preheat the oven to 350 degrees.

2.   Crack eggs into a high-capacity blender. Add carrots, green beans, and onion. Mix until blended into a liquid. I received a Vitamix as a gift and I love it, but any high-speed food processor or blender should work just fine.

3.   In a large mixing bowl, mix the veggie-egg mixture with the meat and breadcrumbs. Have your child mix with their hands; some kids will hate this, others will love it.

4. Line the baking sheet with unbleached parchment paper to make clean up easier. Make three loaves out of the mixture and place on the baking sheet.

5. Spread the tomato paste on the top and sides with a spreader or butter knife.

6. Bake in the oven for an hour.

Pack a Lunch

When you have a child with food allergies or dietary restrictions, you know you are stuck packing school lunches every day.

If you've tried it before, you know that gluten-free bread is, well, not fabulous, and Leo agrees. Leo doesn't prefer to eat sandwiches for this reason and that is quite okay by me. Really, no one needs all that bread every day, gluten-free or otherwise. Even gluten-free breads made with rice flour have refined sugar, causing the same effects as any starch would to your system. Sugar spikes and yeast feeds when you consume rice-based products. While many gluten substitutes are available now, some may not be beneficial to your health. In fact, if you load your child up on gluten-free breads and cookies, you will not be nurturing a healthy gut; instead, you will be feeding them yeast and bad bacteria. It's a good idea to keep your gluten-free replacement foods, such as bread, pasta, and especially sweets, to a minimum.

If you're not packing sandwiches for lunch, what do you pack? Pack leftovers, I say! Whenever we cook, I plan ahead to make sure there will be leftovers for lunch. Save yourself the trouble and keep lunch low in refined sugars. Pack fruits and raw veggies for snacks. Fruit is a superior choice compared to sugars and carbs.

It's funny—Leo's teachers always comment on his "gourmet lunches." I have to admit that I am certainly not a gourmet cook. Most people are just not accustomed to children bringing in a hot lunch meal, so it seems "gourmet" to them, I suppose. Most importantly, Leo is happy with his lunches. It is one less meal to plan and prepare for us and much healthier than the alternatives. It's a win-win for leftovers!

Or if you *need* to pack a cold lunch for a field trip or the likes . . .

THE FLYNN-WICH

Flynn is our friend who has a severe peanut allergy. Flynn is extremely intelligent and is very aware of his and other children's food allergies. Flynn is a fabulous and attentive host. Flynn is always thoughtful and helps Leo avoid his food allergies when they eat together. Flynn came up with this great lunch alternative to having a PB&J or grilled cheese. Flynn made a sandwich for his hungry little brother Charlie while demonstrating the recipe!

The Goods

- ♥ 2 slices of your choice of gluten-free bread
- ♥ Spicy or yellow gluten-free mustard (Trader Joe's is gluten-free)
- ♥ 2 gluten-free lunch meats of your choice (we like to use Applegate Organics because their products are gluten-, soy-, and dairy-free)

Applegate lunch meat ingredients: Organic turkey, water. Contains less than 2 percent of the following: sea salt, organic honey, organic cane sugar, celery powder.

Putting Everything Together

1. Lay out two pieces of gluten-free bread.

2. Squeeze gluten-free mustard on both pieces of bread and spread with a butter knife or the back of a spoon.

3. Arrange organic, preservative-free lunch meat (or fresh gluten-free meats from your local deli) by placing one type of lunch meat on one slice of bread and another type of meat on the other slice.

4. Put the sides together, cut in triangles, and remove crusts if you prefer (Flynn and Scarlett like the crusts cut off).

VERNACCHIO SAUSAGE AND PEPPERS

Even though I come from a family with an Italian side (Leo's father is Italian, too), no sausage and peppers recipe was passed down to me. I made this one up myself. It is naturally free of most common food allergens.

The Goods

- ♥ 3 small 1-lb packages sweet Italian sausage links
- ♥ 9 organic red, orange, and yellow peppers (I don't think green are sweet enough)
- ♥ 2 organic sweet onions
- ♥ 3 tbsp organic high-heat cooking oil
- ♥ 1 tsp organic garlic salt
- ♥ 1 tsp organic crushed garlic
- ♥ 4 large shakes dried organic basil
- ♥ 3–4 soft shakes Herbes de Provence (I think it's the best ingredient in the dish)

My father discovered an amazing sweet Italian sausage that I like to use at Trader Joe's. He was a Trader Joe's fanatic long before it became big. For months on end, all I heard was, "You have to go to Trader Joe's!"

Putting Everything Together

1. Preheat the oven to 375 degrees.

2. Cut sausage links into 1-inch pieces with scissors.

3. Roughly chop the peppers and onions. I like to keep them large since they tend to shrink a lot. You want your dish chunky.

4. Mix the sausage, peppers, and onions in a large glass or ceramic casserole dish.

5. Mix in the oil and dry spices until evenly coated.

6. Cook for 40 minutes, mixing periodically to prevent the edges of the peppers and onions from burning. A little browning is good.

I like to use scissors to cut my food, wherever possible. It is one of the best discoveries I've ever made! It also saves you from the tired hands that come with always having to cut your children's food when they are too young to help. Once they are ready to cut food by themselves, let them. It is a great skill that nurtures independence.

This dish goes well with gluten-free fusilli that has been tossed with organic olive oil and a little garlic salt.

EVERY JEWISH MOTHER'S POTTED CHICKEN

My mother and her friends always made this dish when I was growing up. Their mothers, in turn, made it for them. It is a very traditional dish, and naturally allergen-free!

The Goods

- ♥ 3 lb whole organic chicken, washed and dried
- ♥ 1 tbsp organic high-heat cooking oil
- ♥ 1 tsp fine organic sea salt
- ♥ 1 tsp organic black pepper
- ♥ 3 stalks organic celery with leafy parts, peeled and chopped
- ♥ 1 parsnip, peeled and chopped
- ♥ ½ bag organic baby carrots, peeled and chopped
- ♥ 1 large organic onion, chopped
- ♥ 2 bay leaves, whole
- ♥ 3 sprigs fresh thyme, chopped
- ♥ 4 cloves organic garlic, quartered
- ♥ Rosemary, chopped or whole according to your preference
- ♥ 2 tbsp organic parsley, chopped
- ♥ 1 tsp organic paprika

To make shopping quicker, buy a soup starter pack in the produce section in your grocery store. It should contain ingredients like parsley, parsnip, and dill. Some markets carry starter packs that cater especially to Jewish clientele.

Putting Everything Together

1. Cut the chicken in pieces; I always cut the breasts in half. Remove the skin if you prefer or remove it after cooking, as the rendering fat will give the dish flavor.

2. Add oil to a frying pan and add the chicken to brown. Salt and pepper to taste.

3. Arrange the chicken, chopped vegetables, and fresh spices in a medium-large Dutch oven or a Crock-Pot.

4. Add filtered water about one-third of the way up so that most of the ingredients are covered in water.

5. Add a bit more salt, pepper, and the paprika.

6. Cover and cook over low heat for 2 hours. Check occasionally to see if more water needs to be added.

7. Serve right out of the pot.

I Can't Keep Calm
Because
I Have a Jewish Mother

Optional: Adding a little ketchup can make this dish sweeter. My mom used to do this, but I like it without ketchup. If you do, be sure to use a gluten-free, low-sugar organic ketchup like the one Annie's makes.

MENA'S QUICK SPAGHETTI SAUCE

Sadly, my children never got to meet Mena, their great-grandmother. Luckily, they get to enjoy her most treasured recipe.

The Goods

- ♥ 3 tablespoons organic olive oil
- ♥ 4 cans organic peeled plum tomatoes
- ♥ 3 cloves organic garlic, peeled and sliced in chunks
- ♥ 3 cans organic tomato paste
- ♥ 2 tablespoons organic dried crushed basil
- ♥ 3 teaspoons organic sea salt
- ♥ 2 tablespoons organic sugar
- ♥ 2 bay leaves
- ♥ 3 cans filtered water (use the empty tomato paste cans)

Putting Everything Together

1. In a large sauce pot, heat the oil on low heat.

2. Pour the tomatoes into a large bowl. Use a potato masher to mash and puree the tomatoes finely. This is a great job for the kids. Set aside.

3. Add the sliced garlic cloves to the heated oil. Sauté the garlic for about 5 minutes. Be careful not to burn the garlic.

4. Add in tomato paste and crushed basil. Continue to cook on low heat, stirring constantly, for about 15 minutes.

5. Add the pureed tomatoes to the tomato paste mixture and mix.

6. Add in the salt to taste, as well as the sugar and bay leaves.

7. Pour the filtered water into the pot, and cover and simmer on medium-low heat until the sauce begins to boil.

8. Slide the lid off, leaving the pot partially uncovered to let some steam out. Continue to cook for another 1½ hours.

BAKED ZITI PARTY

The Goods

- ♥ 1 box organic gluten-free ziti
- ♥ 1 jar tomato basil sauce (or substitute 1½ cups of Mena's Quick Spaghetti Sauce (see recipe on p. 99)
- ♥ 1 tsp organic dried basil
- ♥ 1 tsp organic dried oregano
- ♥ 2 cups vegan dairy-free mozzarella cheese (Daiya makes a lot of great vegan cheese options)
- ♥ Organic garlic salt, to taste

Putting Everything Together

1. Preheat the oven to 350 degrees.

2. Cook the pasta and strain. It is a good idea to rinse rice pasta under cool water after cooking to avoid sticking. I also add a drop of olive oil to keep it slippery.

3. Mix pasta, sauce, basil, oregano, and 1 cup of your dairy-free mozzarella into a large glass baking dish or baking tin if the food is traveling. Mix well, but be careful not to break the pasta apart. Gluten-free pasta can be fragile.

4. Sprinkle the remaining cup of dairy-free mozzarella on top.

5. Sprinkle a little garlic salt over the top of the mozzarella.

6. Bake in the oven for about 30 minutes or until slightly browned and bubbly.

Normally, I don't like to use any tins or aluminum foil. However, if you are bringing this dish to a party, don't beat yourself up for using a disposable casserole tin. The world won't end, and party-goers won't be poisoned. It's okay, once in a while. We can't be perfect all of the time!

The last time I brought this dish to someone's house, the children and parents gobbled it up. The kids actually chose this over the chicken fingers and fries.

IF IT LOOKS LIKE MAC AND CHEESE . . .

This was the first recipe Leo actually learned to make. A therapist working with Leo made a visual shopping list and visual recipe that he could follow to complete the entire task. Afterward, Leo and his therapist sat down and shared the meal they had made together. Leo loved this. He felt proud of the whole thing.

Leo did a great job looking for the items at the market. It helps to keep him focused to have a list. We took pictures of the actual products we were going to use, rather than just a general picture of the items. That is a good way to start, but when you want your child to generalize the concepts, you can use more generic photos to expand their understanding. This way they won't get stuck if one item is not available that day and you need to find a substitute.

Generalization is a hard concept for many children with autism. Our kids can be very rigid in their interpretations of things and the world. Shopping and cooking is a great way to demonstrate generalization, and your child will begin to recognize the concept of his or her food allergies and what foods they should substitute instead.

The Goods

- ♥ 2 cups gluten-free pasta (elbows, shells, or whatever your child likes)
- ♥ 2 tbsp vegan/dairy-free butter
- ♥ 1½ cups dairy-free cheddar cheese (You can substitute the ½ cup with mozzarella or another kind of vegan cheese to mix it up)
- ♥ Organic salt, to taste
- ♥ Organic pepper, to taste

Putting Everything Together

1. Cook the pasta according to the directions. Keep it a bit al dente.

2. Remove the pasta and lower the heat on the burner. Drain the pasta, but save about a cup of cooked pasta water to add back in later. Do not rinse the pasta.

3. Return the pot to the stovetop and add in butter, melting over low heat.

4. Return the pasta to the pot. Stir the butter into the pasta until the pasta is coated.

5. Slowly stir in about half of the reserved pasta water and the shredded cheese, mixing frequently and gently. Continue adding more pasta water until the desired thickness is achieved. The sauce should be smooth.

6. Sprinkle in salt and pepper to taste.

7. Remove pot from heat and let it sit for about 5 minutes.

You can always add some chopped organic broccoli or peas to give the dish color and more nutritional value. I think this is the most difficult dish to do allergy-free because its natural components are gluten and dairy. But it will have to do if your child is a big mac and cheese lover. Mac and cheese is such a staple for kids, especially toddlers, so it's nice to have this option in your repertoire.

"RICE KRISPIE" BONE-IN PORK CHOPS

The Goods

- 4–6 natural bone-in pork chops, washed and dried
- 2 free-range organic eggs (optional)
- Organic high-heat cooking oil, to drizzle
- 1 cup gluten-free "Krispie Crumbs" breadcrumbs (see recipe on p. 108)

Putting Everything Together

1. Preheat the oven to 350 degrees.

2. Dip the pork chops in egg prior to battering them, or just drizzle a little oil over them for a quicker method. It doesn't make much difference. Leo really likes cracking eggs, so we use eggs most of the time.

3. Put your "Krispie Crumbs" in a large ziplock baggie and place the pork chops in the bag one at a time and shake.

4. Drizzle a bit of oil on top.

5. Cook for about 35 minutes. The internal temperature for the cooked pork should be 145 degrees.

Bone-in is so much better, flavor-wise. Be careful not to overcook the pork chops; I did that for years. The chops should cook for 35 minutes max. Meats continue to cook a little longer after you remove them from the oven. I was the queen of asking everyone, "Does this look pink?" for many years.

EZ GLUTEN-FREE BREADCRUMBS

The Goods

- ♥ 1 loaf gluten-free bread (stale is better)
- ♥ 1 tbsp organic garlic salt
- ♥ 1 tsp organic fine sea salt
- ♥ 1 tsp organic black pepper
- ♥ Organic paprika, to taste (optional; this sweet spice is good for fried chicken)

Putting Everything Together

1. Toast the bread and cut into smaller pieces.

2. Place the bread in a high-speed blender (for this, I love my Vitamix!). Start on a lower speed until pieces become smaller and loose.

3. Add the spices. Blend on medium speed until you achieve "crumbs" that are the size you like. Try not to blend it too much or the mixture will be too fine. You may have to use a spoon to dislodge the crumbs that end up at the bottom below the blades.

Leo loves anything with "bread" on it. I think it gives kids the illusion that they are eating something that would be served at a fast-food restaurant, except that's definitely not the case!

ITALIAN-STYLE GLUTEN-FREE BREADCRUMBS

The Goods

- ♥ 1 loaf gluten-free bread (stale is better)
- ♥ 1 tsp dried organic oregano
- ♥ 1 tsp dried organic basil
- ♥ 1 tsp dried organic parsley
- ♥ 1 tsp dried organic thyme
- ♥ 1 tsp dried organic rosemary
- ♥ 1 tbsp organic garlic salt
- ♥ 1 tsp organic black pepper

Putting Everything Together

1. Toast the bread and cut into smaller pieces.

2. Place in high-speed blender.

3. Start on a lower speed until pieces become smaller and loose. Add the spices in a few batches by stopping the blender after a minute or so to add at intervals, so they are evenly distributed.

4. Blend on medium speed until crumbs are fine and well blended, or at the size you like. Dislodge any crumbs that end up at the bottom below the blades with a spoon.

Spice-wise, you can add whatever you like to your breadcrumbs, depending on the kind of dish you're making. Substitute Italian spices for Herbes de Provence for French-style breadcrumbs or brown sugar for a sweet Southern flavor.

KRISPIE CRUMBS

The Goods

- ♥ 2 cups organic gluten-free Rice Krispies cereal
- ♥ 1 tbsp organic garlic salt
- ♥ 1 tsp organic fine sea salt
- ♥ 1 tsp organic black pepper
- ♥ 1 tsp organic paprika (optional)

Putting Everything Together

1. Mix the cereal and spices into your blender.

2. Start slow and gradually increase the speed to medium; don't set the speed on high. You want these a bit larger than the other breadcrumbs; they should stay crunchy.

Make a large batch and keep in a container in the fridge. Though it's a pretty quick recipe, I always get a little happy feeling whenever I remember I already have leftover breadcrumbs in the fridge! It means one less step. Coat chicken, fish, and vegetables with breadcrumbs—they're especially great on artichokes.

ALL SUMMER LONG

All-American BBQ

You cannot go wrong with a summer barbecue of burgers and dogs. It is an American family right! Sorry to kill your BBQ buzz, but hot dogs, of course, are likely one of the most processed and unhealthiest things you can eat that are filled with who-knows-what. I don't even think I'd call a hot dog food; a better name might be "food product." I guarantee that you will never be able to stop your kids from wanting hot dogs, so don't fight it—just pick out better dogs.

Most hot dogs contain milk or casein. You can find kosher hot dogs that are dairy-free, but these still have a bunch of other additives and junk that you want to avoid. Look for organic hot dogs with no additives and no nitrates. Applegate makes a variety of beef, chicken, and turkey dogs that I like.

We do bun-less barbecues. The extra carbohydrates that come from eating bread, gluten-free or not, will turn into sugars that contribute to many health issues. You don't need buns; your kids will get used to it. This will just become the way your family eats at a barbecue.

Cheeseburgers? Nope . . . and that's no big deal! Use organic ground meat and spruce them up with a little organic garlic salt, kosher salt, and pepper for your burgers, but skip the cheese. Even if your child isn't allergic to dairy, cheese is really an unnecessary food.

Many folks, including myself, love cheese. Cheese is wonderful; it ranges from overly processed to artisanal and has become a staple in the American diet. However, cheese doesn't have unique nutritional properties that can't be found in other non-dairy foods, even vegetables. You don't *need* cheese for any type of dietary nutrition. It's really just a superfluous thing we eat because we relish it. Skip the cheese at home, but enjoy it once in a while when you dine out without your kids.

Pair your American barbecue burgers and dogs with Erica's Heirloom Tomato Avocado Salad (p. 144). I like to put salad on top of my burger. You can certainly find gluten-free and organic condiments to complete this American experience. Make some Rooty Fries (see recipe on p. 138) or Sweet Rooties (see recipe on p. 135) in the oven while you grill.

When you make these minor adjustments, you can still partake in an all-American barbecue experience that will be much healthier and free from common food allergens.

CHICKEN ON THE BARBIE

The Goods

♥ Homemade organic BBQ sauce
- 1 cup organic gluten-free ketchup
- ¼ cup gluten-free white vinegar
- ¼ cup organic dark brown sugar
- 2 tbsp organic dried paprika
- 1 tbsp organic cooking oil
- 1 tsp organic chili powder
- 2 tsp organic garlic powder
- 2 tbsp organic dark honey

♥ Mixed organic chicken legs, thighs, and breasts, washed and dried

♥ Organic sea salt and black pepper

Putting Everything Together

1. Combine the ingredients for your BBQ sauce. You can also buy BBQ sauces at the market that are natural, organic, and gluten-free.

2. Cut the large chicken breasts into smaller pieces for an even cook time. Salt and pepper the chicken, and smother in BBQ sauce.

3. Place the chicken on the grill to cook. Brush more sauce on as you cook. Try to keep the grill closed so you don't slow down the cooking. It should take about 30 to 40 minutes.

CORN ON THE COB

Corn can be a nightmare for children with gastrointestinal issues and adults with diverticulitis, for that matter. In addition to being high in sugar, corn is the most genetically modified, overtreated crop around. Having said all that, Leo absolutely loves corn. We cannot have it in the house without him obsessing over it.

Once or twice in the summer, I allow Leo to eat corn and I know that his behavior will become erratic afterwards. It's just one of those foods he is not specifically allergic to; however, he will get a bad behavioral reaction to it. Sometimes, I just want to see his happy face gobbling up good old corn on the cob. Once in a while, it's okay to let your child enjoy something that might not be the best thing for them. If you don't, it will likely become a source of anxiety for your child.

The Goods

♥ Corn on the cob, as many as you need

Putting Everything Together

1. Remove the silk and only the top few husks. You want to cook corn in the husk for maximum flavor. My kids love cleaning corn.

2. Soak the corn in the husk in cold water for about 15 minutes to provide moisture for cooking and keep the husks from burning on the grill.

3. Grill the corn on the top shelf of the grill for about 20 minutes.

4. Let sit until it's cool enough to remove the remaining husks.

This is important: you do not need to put anything on the corn—no seasoning, salt, or butter. If the corn is good, it will be delicious in its natural state with the smoky flavor of the grill. Always eat corn on the cob with your hands, or you can get some fun corn holders (we used to have the corn-shaped ones). Just give your child an enzyme and be prepared for corn mania afterward!

FARMERS' MARKET GRILLED VEGGIES

The Goods

- ♥ 6 mixed organic peppers
- ♥ 2 small organic onions
- ♥ 1 whole eggplant
- ♥ Organic squash, zucchini, or whatever else you can find at your local farmers' market
- ♥ 1 tbsp organic cooking oil
- ♥ 1 tsp organic sea salt
- ♥ 1 tsp organic black peppercorns

Putting Everything Together

1. Wash and chop the vegetables into large chunks.

2. Place the chopped vegetables in a large grill pan with a handle. Drizzle with oil, salt, and pepper.

3. Close the grill and cook for about 30 minutes on medium heat, mixing occasionally.

ONE SIDE IS
ENOUGH

The Truth About Starch

As an American society, we have become nutritionally conditioned to think that we need to have three different varieties of foods on our plate at dinnertime: a protein, a vegetable, and a starch.

Generally, there is a lot of mixed information out there about starches and carbs. When we talk about starches, we need to be aware of yeast, and it is important to remember that yeast feeds on sugar. A diet high in carbs will create yeast in an unbalanced gut, an issue that can be exacerbated in a child with gastrointestinal issues.

All vegetables and fruits, even those that are not starchy like potatoes, contain carbohydrates. You *can* get all of the carbs you need from vegetables and fruits that are not starches. In that case, why obsess over creating three different types of dishes per meal when you can focus on creating a single healthy, nutritious side?

A Note About Yeast

We all need a balance of bacteria in our guts. However, there are good bacteria and bad bacteria (yeast). Bad bacteria can build up in our bodies if our immune system is not working properly. This is usually common in all types of gastrointestinal distress.

A healthy gut contains good bacteria and bad bacteria in harmony. Children with autism who often have gastrointestinal and immune (allergy) issues are at risk of their guts being out of balance when there is an overgrowth of yeast. When bad bacteria or yeast overgrows, it takes over the good gut bacteria and this can cause GI and behavioral mayhem. If your child has yeast overgrowth, it can manifest itself in problematic physical and behavioral symptoms, especially in a child that cannot communicate.

Right before Leo had his "autistic regression," he had been on three different varieties of antibiotics for an ear infection that just wouldn't go away. Sound familiar? Yes, we need antibiotics to kill bacteria, but antibiotics remove both bad and good bacteria and can actually cause yeast flares even in otherwise healthy people. This is made worse if you have a dysfunctional immune system or gastrointestinal distress, which may ultimately lead to yeast overgrowth. So, it follows that diet can have a tremendous influence on health and behavior. If you have a healthy immune system and healthy gut, your body should be able to keep yeast at bay.

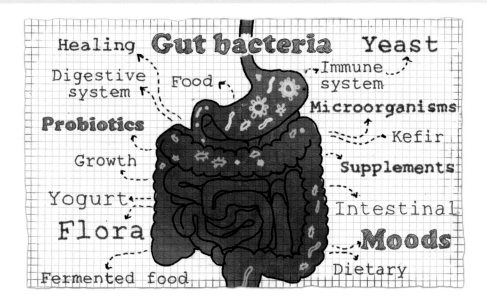

When we talk about starches, it is important to remember that yeast feeds on sugar. A diet high in carbs such as fries, sugar, and fried foods will create yeast in an unbalanced gut. Isn't that the kind of diet most kids eat these days—chicken fingers, French fries, cookies, snacks with processed carbohydrates, and sugary yogurts? Our kids may even crave these foods because their little systems are having a crash and they want more sugar. This is why many children with gastrointestinal distress, food allergies, or behavioral problems do well on diets that are low in or free from carbohydrates. When Leo's gut was at its worst, he needed a diet like the Specific Carbohydrate Diet (SCD), created by the amazing Elaine Gottschall. Unfortunately, many low-carb diets focus on nuts. Since Leo has a nut allergy, his diet had to be even more restricted, specialized, and compensated with supplements.

Here are some things you can look for if you suspect your child may have yeast overgrowth:

- Thrush in the mouth or on the skin

- Eczema

- Diaper rash or rashes in the joint areas

- Sleep problems

- Spacey-ness

- Highs and lows including random crying and laughing

- Hyperactivity and attention problems

- Aggression

- Increased stimming or sensory-seeking behaviors

- Sugar cravings

- Gastrointestinal distress, such as constipation

Initially, Leo exhibited all of these symptoms. Even now when I get sloppy with his diet, I will notice these symptoms flaring up and I will tweak his diet to address it. You may hear your doctor say something like, "Well, that's just autism . . ." I say find a new doctor then! I have witnessed with my own eyes how much the foods Leo eats affect his health and his behavior. Testing for yeast is available, of course, but as his mother, I've learned to observe Leo's behavior and symptoms and I can know without having to go to the doctor when he is having a yeast flare-up.

LEO'S ITALIAN ARTICHOKES

Have you ever met a child who likes artichokes? Not really. However, kids like anything you put breadcrumbs on. My mom always made artichokes when we were kids; it was part of her Italian vegetable repertoire. In fact, my parents were the ones who first introduced artichokes to my children. Now we have another traditional and healthy family food that we can all enjoy together.

The Goods

- ♥ 4 large artichokes
- ♥ ½ tsp organic garlic salt
- ♥ 1 cup EZ Gluten-Free Breadcrumbs (see recipe on p. 106)
- ♥ 4 tsp organic Italian olive oil

Artichokes are always fun to make. Here's how to prepare them:

1. First, take the artichoke by the stem and bang it firmly on the counter until the leaves spread apart. Don't hit too hard or the leaves may break. Remove the bottom outer stems and any stems that are brownish. Artichokes are prickly, so be careful when working with them.

2. If your child is good with scissors, have him or her sit at the table and cut the tips off the leaves into a trash bag on the floor. This may require supervision, but it will keep them focused for quite some time. It is also good practice for fine motor skills.

3. Cut the artichokes in half and cut the stems off.

4. I like to remove the inner hairy, prickly leaves that surround the heart before I cook them so you can eat everything straightaway without worrying that your child might accidentally consume the prickly inner leaves. My kids are always shouting, "More heart! More heart!" and I like to save myself the anxiety of removing the leaves after cooking. You can actually gag if you swallow this stuff; it feels like getting a hair caught in your throat. Carefully slice the top choke right above the heart, making sure to scrape out the hairs and purple leaves above. It is easier to remove this area after the artichokes are cooked because it is softer, but the process is a lot messier.

Putting Everything Together

1. Fill the bottom of a large, covered pot with a bit of water. Place the artichokes in the pot so they are partially submerged at the bottom.

2. Sprinkle garlic salt and breadcrumbs evenly over the artichokes, making sure to get the seasonings in between the leaves. Drizzle with olive oil.

3. Cover and cook over medium-high heat for at least an hour. Smaller artichokes may take less time.

4. I like to put the artichokes under the broiler very briefly when they are done to crisp up the breadcrumbs. Gluten-free breadcrumbs can sometimes be more soggy than wheat breadcrumbs, so it's a good thing that this last step can fix it!

Artichokes are a lot of fun to eat. You can eat them with your hands, and it gets messy. I am amazed by their anatomy; they are unlike any other vegetable.

It's funny—I have met grown men who won't try an artichoke. I laugh to myself whenever my kids eat them in front of an adult. Plus one for my rock star eaters!

PICKLE THIEF'S PICKLES

Being Jewish, we often go to the deli for pickles. Most of the foods at our local Jewish deli are allergen-free. On deli nights, Leo steals all of the pickles!

Here's how to make your own pickles.

The Goods

♥ 1 lb medium cucumbers, cut into spears or slices

♥ 3 cloves garlic

♥ ½ tsp rainbow peppercorns

♥ ½ tsp whole mustard seed

♥ 1 tsp fresh dill weed

♥ 1 whole dried bay leaf

♥ 6½ tbsp gluten-free white distilled vinegar

♥ 6½ tbsp gluten-free white wine vinegar

♥ ¾ cup filtered water

Putting Everything Together

1. Put the cut cucumbers in a 2-quart jar with a lid.

2. Add the garlic, peppercorns, mustard seed, dill weed, and bay leaf.

3. Stir the vinegars and water together.

4. Pour the vinegar mixture over the cucumbers and shake the jar well to combine.

5. Cover and chill in the refrigerator for at least 24 hours. Your pickles will keep up to 3 months in the refrigerator.

If you like a sweeter bread and butter-style pickle, add ⅔ cup of light brown organic sugar. Bread and butter pickles are *my* favorite pickles, though Leo definitely prefers them salty and tangy!

EAT AS MUCH KRAUT AS YOU LIKE

I have no idea why, but Leo *loves* sauerkraut! I tend to think it's his gut calling out for probiotics, which exist in all fermented foods. It may also just be the strong and tangy buzz his taste buds get. Either way, who cares! It is strange and beautiful—my Leo and his sauerkraut!

Most sauerkraut sold in supermarkets and shops is pasteurized to give it a longer shelf life. Beneficial bacteria are destroyed during pasteurization. To keep its nutritional benefits, sauerkraut should be made the traditional way and enjoyed raw. A single serving of raw sauerkraut provides more health benefits than traditional probiotic drinks or supplements.

The Goods

- ♥   2 medium organic green cabbage heads
- ♥   1½ tbsp kosher salt

You'll need two glass mixing bowls that fit one inside the other, and something heavy to rest inside the smaller bowl like a stone or paperweight. Another option is to use mason jars and a smaller jam jar that fits inside. A supply of mason jars is always good to have on hand.

All your materials need to be sanitized to avoid the growth of unwanted bacteria that might mess with the good bacteria during the fermentation process.

Putting Everything Together

1. Remove the large outer leaves of the cabbage and set aside.

2. Core and shred the cabbage as thinly as possible.

3. As you shred the cabbage, place it in layers in the larger glass bowl or mason jar. Add bits of salt in between the layers. The salt pulls the moisture from the cabbage, creating the brine that the kraut will culture in.

4. Get the culture process moving by pressing down on the cabbage with your hands. Do this for about 5 minutes. It is a fun activity for the kids.

5. Arrange the outer leaves on top to make a layer of coverage for your kraut.

6. Now, place the smaller glass bowl or jam jar on top and weigh it down with a stone, a paperweight, or even a heavy vegetable. Both the containers must be sanitized and they should fit tightly, one inside the other.

7. Leave the mixture out in the kitchen to ferment. Depending on the climate, the temperature in your kitchen, and any other factor that affects bacteria growth, it may take anywhere from three to seven days to ferment.

8. Check it daily to see how things are coming. You can remove any mold that forms on top.

9. To know when your kraut is done fermenting, look for bubbling, a sour but pleasant smell, and desired taste. When those things are achieved, transfer your kraut into glass sealable jars or keep it in the mason jar and put in the fridge to store.

I suggest making sauerkraut in smaller batches until you get the hang of it. Once you are comfortable with the fermentation process, you can make larger batches by increasing the ingredients proportionately, using larger bowls and jars, or even purchasing fermentation crocks.

YOU HAD ME AT BACON . . . MORE PEAS, PLEASE

Bacon makes everything taste better! Cooking bacon gives off that familiar smell that invokes a pleasant "hunger vibe" in the house. Hopefully, your kids will be hypnotized into eating peas by this bacon effect.

The Goods

- ♥ 6 strips organic nitrate- and dairy-free bacon (brands like Welshire and Applegate are good options)
- ♥ 2 tsp organic shallot or onion, finely chopped
- ♥ 1 bag frozen organic peas

Putting Everything Together

1. Cut the bacon into smaller strips or pieces. Fry slightly over medium heat in a large frying pan.

2. Add the finely chopped shallot or onion to the pan and fry until browned.

3. Add in the peas and fry for about 5 more minutes.

RAINBOW ROASTED VEGGIES

This dish is so much fun to me! It's like a work of art. Your child likely won't eat or even try *all* of the different veggies in this dish, but don't give up—the next time, they just might.

The Goods

- 2 organic green peppers
- 2 organic red peppers
- 2 organic orange peppers
- 2 organic yellow peppers
- Small organic purple cauliflower
- Medium-large purple onion
- 2 organic green zucchinis
- 6 organic rainbow blend carrots
- 2 yellow organic squashes
- 1 tbsp organic cooking oil
- 1 tsp organic garlic salt
- 1 tsp cracked organic rainbow peppercorns
- 1 tsp Herbes de Provence

Putting Everything Together

1. Preheat the oven to 350 degrees.

2. Wash, peel, core, and cut the veggies into large pieces. Keep in mind that they will shrink considerably during the roasting process.

3. Mix the veggies evenly in a large roasting pan.

4. Add the oil, salt, pepper, and Herbes de Provence.

5. Roast in the oven at 350 degrees for about 45 minutes, mixing every so often. The veggies should be slightly browned on the edges. If they aren't browned, you can switch to broil for a few minutes at the end of the cooking to get the same effect. In the summer, you can use the grill—just be sure to use a veggie pan for the grill.

ITALIAN-FRENCH GREEN BEANS

The Goods

- ♥ 1 lb fresh or frozen organic haricot verts (French green beans)
- ♥ Organic extra virgin olive oil
- ♥ Organic garlic salt, to taste

I prefer to use French green beans aka haricot verts instead of the shorter, pre-cut green beans. Anything that looks closer to food in its natural state is not just a lesson in a farm-to-table lifestyle; it also means it is less processed.

Putting Everything Together

1. If using fresh green beans, wash and snip the ends off.

2. Place green beans in a colander that fits in a medium saucepan. Fill the pan with enough water to reach just under the colander. Cover the pan and steam the beans on medium-low heat for about 10 minutes. Make sure they stay green and are not overcooked.

3. Remove the pan from heat. Pour out the remaining water and remove the colander. Be careful, this is not a job for kids because the colander will be very hot.

4. Place green beans in the pot to sauté. Drizzle in olive oil, sprinkle garlic salt, and mix gently with tongs until the beans are fully cooked but not brown and soggy.

You can add fresh, crushed garlic to this dish if you like. Garlic has been linked with health benefits such as the ability to cure common colds, lower blood pressure, and reduce the risk of heart disease. I use garlic salt in this recipe for our routine meals because it's faster and easier. However, it's nice to use fresh garlic if you're serving this meal to guests during a holiday dinner.

VEGGIE S-GHETTI

Being Italian, our family traditionally ate a lot of spaghetti. If you simply replace your "gluten" with gluten-free pasta, you would end up replacing one starch for another—wheat for rice pasta. Here is a non-starch veggie version that we love at our house!

The Goods

- ♥ 3 tbsp organic high-heat cooking oil
- ♥ 1 organic garlic clove, minced
- ♥ ½ lb organic zucchini "spaghetti-ed"
- ♥ ½ lb organic yellow squash "spaghetti-ed"
- ♥ ½ organic lemon
- ♥ Pinch of organic sea salt
- ♥ Organic rainbow or black peppercorns, to taste

To "spaghetti" your vegetables, use a spiralizer or buy vegetables that are already spiralized or pre-cut.

Putting Everything Together

1. Heat oil in medium-sized saucepan over medium heat.

2. Add minced garlic to the oil and brown slightly.

3. Add your "spaghetti-ed" zucchini and squash and sauté for about 10 minutes, mixing occasionally with tongs.

4. Squeeze lemon, and add salt and pepper toward the end of cooking.

5. Serve as a side dish or main dish!

SWEET ROOTIES

You can use whatever root vegetables you like. The salty and sweet versions work well with different meals. Serve with burgers or meatloaf.

The Goods

- ♥ 3 medium organic sweet potatoes
- ♥ 3 medium organic yams
- ♥ ¾ lb white carrots
- ♥ ¼ cup organic high-heat cooking oil
- ♥ 2 tbsp organic cinnamon sugar mix (1 tbsp cinnamon mixed with 1 tbsp sugar)
- ♥ 1 tsp organic cinnamon
- ♥ 1 tbsp organic light brown sugar

Putting Everything Together

1. Preheat the oven to 400 degrees.

2. Peel and cut the sweet potatoes, yams, and carrots into thick strips. It's very helpful to have a French fry cutter to do this part; it will make your fries sturdy so they won't fall apart.

3. Line a baking sheet with unbleached parchment paper. Place the vegetables in a single layer on the parchment-covered tray.

4. Drizzle oil over the vegetables. Sprinkle or crack cinnamon sugar over evenly.

5. Cook root vegetables for about 30 minutes, turning occasionally.

6. Remove from the oven. Sprinkle the extra cinnamon and brown sugar on top and put back in the oven for another 5 to 10 minutes. Be careful not to drop clumps of cinnamon or brown sugar; try to spread it finely and evenly.

Root Veggies Rock

Root vegetables are likely the most underappreciated foods around. Perhaps some shoppers shy away from them because they look funny and can be intimidating. What do I do with this funny-looking plant? How on earth do I cook this? My kids will never eat something that looks like this! Sound familiar? You are not alone. But don't be quick to pass by these strange and wonderful-looking veggies because root vegetables *rock*!

Root vegetables are vegetables that grow underground, such as beets, carrots, onions, garlic, radishes, turnips, and parsnips. They are packed with health benefits because they absorb super dense nutrients from the underground soil. Root veggies are high in antioxidants and slow-burning fibers. They promote excretion of toxins and steady blood sugar levels and are a great substitute to traditional starchy vegetables like white potatoes.

I think that root vegetables are funky and fabulous-looking. They can be added to almost any meal. They bring an especially nice, earthy vibe to soups and stews in the fall and winter. Eating real foods from the earth not only has great health benefits, it also makes us feel as if we are living as Mother Nature intended. It's hip and cool to work with root vegetables. Roots are also easily found during the winter months when more popular vegetables are not in season, so you definitely want to add them to your shopping list.

You can plain roast root vegetables with a bit of oil and salt, or prepare them as a substitute to French fries.

ROOTY FRIES

The Goods

- 1 lb parsnips
- ¾ lb rutabaga
- 3 large carrots (any color you like; heirloom carrots add a nice color)
- ¼ cup organic high-heat cooking oil
- 1 tsp coarse kosher salt
- Organic garlic salt, to taste
- Ground organic black pepper, to taste

Putting Everything Together

1. Preheat the oven to 400 degrees.

2. Peel and cut the parsnips, rutabaga, and carrots into thick strips. It's very helpful to have a French fry cutter to do this part; it will make your fries sturdy so they won't fall apart.

3. Line a baking sheet with unbleached parchment paper. Place the vegetables in a single layer on the parchment-covered tray.

4. Drizzle oil and sprinkle salt, garlic salt, and pepper evenly over the veggies.

5. Cook for about 30 minutes, turning occasionally, until they are nice and brown. Try not to mess with them too much.

NANNY'S SWEET RHUBARB

The Goods

- ♥ 4 large rhubarb stalks, chopped
- ♥ 4 tbsp organic sugar in the raw
- ♥ A couple strawberries, for garnish

Putting Everything Together

1. Bring a medium saucepan that is full of filtered water to a boil.

2. Boil the chopped rhubarb and sugar, uncovered, for about 20 minutes.

3. Let cool and serve with fresh strawberries.

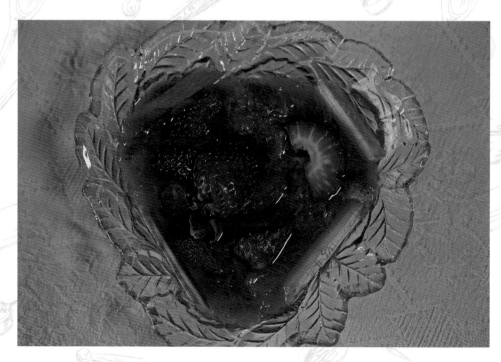

BALSAMIC SHROOMS

There is something about mushrooms that most kids, and even adults, don't like—its texture. The trick is to get moisture out of the mushrooms as much as possible, which will make the shrooms more pleasing to the taste buds. It is important to deal with sensory issues when learning to eat healthy. If your child is averse to the textures of certain veggies, try different preparation methods to change the texture. If that doesn't work, you can always resort to storytelling. I love *Alice in Wonderland*!

The Goods

- ♥ 1–2 tsp organic high-heat cooking oil
- ♥ 2 tsp organic shallot, finely chopped
- ♥ 1½–2 lbs small organic mushrooms (I like using baby bella or white button mushrooms. I buy them pre-sliced and usually pick up two small packages of cut mushrooms; they shrink down a lot after cooking.)
- ♥ Organic sea salt, to taste
- ♥ 2 tsp organic balsamic vinegar

Putting Everything Together

1. Heat the oil over medium heat in a large frying pan.

2. Add in the shallot and fry a minute or two.

3. Add the mushrooms and a pinch of salt to the pan.

4. Sauté the mushrooms for about 3 to 5 minutes over medium heat, stirring frequently, until the mushrooms soften and release moisture.

5. Pour in the balsamic vinegar, stirring frequently, and sauté for another 5 minutes.

LETTUCE HEAD

I tried giving Leo salad and lettuce for years, but he would always push it away. One day, Leo's grandfather prepared salad *with* him, doctoring it up with a little garlic salt, olive oil, and white vinegar, and Leo ate it for the first time. Even though Leo loves lettuce today, he still won't eat salad mixed with other things like tomatoes and shredded carrots, and will usually pick it out and put it on my plate. He will, however, eat oranges in his salad.

Grandpa, as an artist, makes a big deal about creating "the salad." It is a project of nutrition and culinary delight that he can share with the kids. Scarlett takes a lot of pride in making salads. We also like to put fruit in—apples, oranges, blueberries, strawberries, pears, or anything else in the house that is just about to go bad.

Many children with autism take words literally. When you say "lettuce head," they may actually envision a person with a lettuce as a head!

The Goods

- ♥ 1 head organic iceberg lettuce
- ♥ 2 tbsp organic extra virgin olive oil
- ♥ 2 tsp distilled white wine vinegar
- ♥ Organic garlic salt, to taste

Putting Everything Together

1. Wash and chop the lettuce. This is a great job for kids, and you can purchase good knives for children on sites like Amazon.

2. Use a salad spinner to dry the lettuce—it's fun for the kids!

3. In a large salad bowl, toss the lettuce with olive oil and vinegar using tongs. White vinegar has a strong taste, so don't go crazy.

4. Sprinkle in garlic salt to taste.

ERICA'S HEIRLOOM TOMATO AVOCADO SALAD

I absolutely love heirloom tomatoes—how they look, how they taste, and pretty much everything else about them. I prefer the dark purplish ones, but the whole variety of colors, shapes, and flavors of heirlooms give this dish so much character. Heirloom tomatoes can be expensive, so treat yourself once in a while.

The Goods

- ♥ 6–8 mixed heirloom tomatoes
- ♥ 2–3 ripe organic avocados
- ♥ Organic extra virgin olive oil, to drizzle
- ♥ Organic garlic salt, to taste
- ♥ Pinch Herbes de Provence
- ♥ Organic balsamic vinegar, to drizzle

Putting Everything Together

1. Rinse the tomatoes and remove the seeds to keep your tomatoes from being slimy. Chop the tomatoes into bite-sized pieces.

2. Slice the avocados in half, avoiding the pit. Carefully but firmly stick your knife into the pit and wiggle slightly until the pit comes out easily. Scoop the avocado flesh out and slice.

3. Place chopped tomatoes and sliced avocado in a colander. Gently mix, drizzling in olive oil and garlic salt to taste.

4. Sprinkle in a pinch of Herbes de Provence, and drizzle on balsamic vinegar.

5. Mix the salad, being careful not to mush the avocados up too much.

Keep the Kids Busy

Exercise is a critical part of your child's health and routine. We tried soccer and other typical children's sports for years without success. I started boxing about three years ago. Boxing is great for stress relief; it's like occupational therapy in a sport. I just knew Leo would love boxing. It is great for coordination, it provides deep pressure, and you get to hit things! Who doesn't love to hit things?

Leo practices yoga at school. Every morning, his whole class does yoga under their teacher's guidance, and they say "namaste." Leo also loves to swim, ride his bike, take nature walks, horseback ride, and, of course, jump like crazy at BounceU or Sky Zone. His most favorite places in the world are on the beach and in the ocean.

Leo even surfed for the first time last summer in Montauk at Surfers Healing. We definitely found our new favorite beach vacation spot in Montauk, the coolest little surf town on the East Coast!

Fall festivals, forget about it, we hit them all! Scarecrows, hayrides, and pumpkins are too much fun.

Leo really enjoys art and woodworking. He gets super messy, but who can argue with an expression of creativity? Leo also loves to swing and could spend all day on a tree swing staring up at the leaves and the clouds.

Think out of the box. Don't give up, and you will find an activity your child enjoys. It may just be something that you and your child can share together.

And, yes, sometimes we all just want to chill out too!

SOUPS RX

Healing Broth

Hide broth in anything and everything. Once your broths are made, set some aside in the fridge or freezer so you can use it in other recipes. You can give any dish a nutritional boost by adding homemade chicken broth or bone broth. Yes, there is a reason your mom makes soup when you are sick.

GRANDMA'S HEALING CHICKEN SOUP

Some days Leo will eat soup and other days he won't feel like it. However, he loves it when Grandma makes soup. I don't think there is anything more traditional for a Jewish grandmother than to make chicken soup for her family. Grandpa's bowl always gets a whole onion from the soup. My mother never left any chicken in the soup, which I never understood. Instead, she removes the white meat and uses it to make her famous chicken salad (see recipe on p. 158).

The Goods

- ♥ 1½ organic chickens, chopped (you can ask your butcher to cut them for you)
- ♥ 1 bunch organic fresh dill
- ♥ 2 organic celery hearts
- ♥ 2 organic parsnips
- ♥ 5 organic carrots, sliced at an angle
- ♥ 2 organic onions
- ♥ 2 tbsp kosher salt
- ♥ 2 tsp organic garlic salt
- ♥ 2 tsp organic black pepper

Putting Everything Together

1. Wash the cut chicken and place in a large soup pot.

2. Tie the dill, celery hearts, and parsnips together with kitchen string and add to the pot.

3. Fill the pot with filtered water until almost reaching the top.

4. Add the carrot slices and whole onions to the pot.

5. Add in kosher salt, garlic salt, and pepper.

6. Cover the pot and bring to a boil. When the soup starts to boil, skim the top until the froth is gone.

7. Lower to a simmer and prop the lid halfway off. Simmer for 1½ hours.

8. Remove the chicken with tongs and set aside in a glass dish to cool. Add gluten-free egg noodles to the pot before serving.

BEEF BONE BROTH WITH VEGGIE PUREE

At the market, I ask the butcher for bones, specifically marrow- and collagen-heavy bones, which yield a much denser, nutrient-heavy broth that is packed with gelatin. Gelatin is known to help heal leaky gut, benefiting those with inflammatory and autoimmune diseases—that would be Leo. Then, I get out my favorite oversized Le Creuset soup pot, hit the bones, and let the healing begin!

I first learned about bone broth at a TACA (Talk About Curing Autism) meeting when a few of the mothers talked about using it to heal their children's guts. It felt like there was a secret society of moms making and using bone broth like medicine. I was intrigued, and I began reading up and asking anyone I could to tell me about their experience with this strange and almost grotesque-sounding healing juice. People would drink it from to-go mugs and feed it to their children for breakfast, lunch, and dinner.

I then came across a book by Dr. Natasha Campbell-McBride about Gut and Psychology Syndrome, which also describes the GAPS diet, a diet similar to the Specific Carbohydrate Diet, which I already had experience with. Both diets specifically discuss autism and the gut-brain connection. With Leo's tremendous food allergies and sensitivities at the time, I mixed both diets together since he couldn't eat all of the foods from each diet. That was when bone broth came into our house.

The Goods

- ♥ 2 large organic onions, roughly chopped
- ♥ 4 organic carrots, peeled and roughly chopped
- ♥ 3 organic celery stalks, roughly chopped
- ♥ 4 lb marrow- and collagen-heavy beef bones
- ♥ 4 quarts filtered water
- ♥ 2 tbsp organic apple cider vinegar
- ♥ 2 organic garlic cloves, crushed
- ♥ 1 bunch fresh organic parsley

Putting Everything Together

1. Add all of the ingredients into a large pot or slow cooker.

2. Cook on low for 12 to 24 hours.

3. Remove the vegetables from the broth and puree them in a food processor.

4. Serve the soup with pureed vegetables.

Keep and freeze leftover broth to add to vegetables or other dishes for added flavor and a nutrient boost.

GRANDMA'S LEGENDARY CHICKEN SALAD

What do you do with the chicken left over from your chicken soup? Make chicken salad, of course!

The Goods

- ♥ White chicken meat, cooked (from 1½ chickens or Grandma's Healing Chicken Soup on p. 153)
- ♥ 3 heaping tbsp natural or organic mayonnaise (Earth Balance has a great option)
- ♥ 4 organic free-range eggs, hard-boiled, with shells removed
- ♥ 2 organic celery stalks, roughly chopped
- ♥ 2 tsp fine organic sea salt
- ♥ Organic black pepper, to taste (optional)

Putting Everything Together

1. Remove the skin from the chicken and pull apart the flesh. Place chicken meat in a large mixing bowl.

2. Add the mayonnaise to the chicken pieces.

3. Cut the hard-boiled eggs into chunks; keep it chunky, not sliced.

4. Add celery, salt, pepper if you'd like, and hard-boiled eggs. Mix together until well combined.

5. Chill in the refrigerator before serving.

You can make a two-course meal out of the chicken soup and salad. Serve the chicken salad with some gluten-free crackers or toast. You can also serve it with a side of greens or something sweet, like Aunt Jackie's Pineapple Spoon Bread (see recipe on p. 166).

HOLIDAY FARE

Holidays Used to Suck

When Leo and I began the journey of healing his gut, food choices were very limited. Leo was also young; he was very affected by autism and had no idea that he couldn't or shouldn't eat certain foods. Family members did not understand the issue, and at times they would insult me for my choices regarding Leo's diet. They weren't my choices alone—Leo had been under the strict care and supervision of a gastrointestinal physician and a certified nutritionist. I wasn't messing around.

Family holidays were overrun with foods Leo couldn't eat. Platters of pastas, cheeses, and casseroles loaded with butter and milk. Tables filled with candy, nuts, and decadent desserts. It was like bringing a kid to a candy store and telling him he couldn't have anything! I tried to educate family and friends, but they didn't understand. It was a holiday tradition, and that's how they did things. At first, we tried packing along Leo's own food, but he would run around like a Tasmanian devil, grabbing things from all sides of the dinner table and ending up with rashes and stomach complications. He was impossible to keep up with. Eventually, we gave up and stopped attending holiday events.

Leo's father and I would take turns bringing Leo's sister, Scarlett, to family gatherings so she wouldn't have to miss out and could spend time with her cousins, aunts, and uncles. One of us would stay home with Leo (usually me). It was always sad, depressing to be the one who had to stay home on Christmas or Thanksgiving. Imagine that, food could also cause such pain and isolation! I had always wanted to pass on holiday traditions to my children, but it just wasn't happening for my family. The joy of family traditions was dead.

Fortunately, I am a resourceful fighter by nature. Having a child with autism and health issues really threw those parts of my personality into full gear. So it began—I started to experiment on traditional holiday recipes and prepared them without gluten, casein, soy, or nuts. I replaced canned and processed foods with organic and whole foods. Back then, the Internet wasn't filled with information like it is now, so I relied heavily on what I could find at the market. I began fighting my way back to some normalcy and tradition as I started cooking differently. I made holiday dinners at my house instead. The holidays were smaller, but the important people attended. In the beginning, there were two of every dish because my mother would insist on her way of making certain dishes; plus, admittedly, mine didn't taste so great yet. No one wanted to try "Leo's food." So, I learned to make the dishes better and tastier, without using most of the ingredients I had known and eaten growing up. I had to start new family traditions. Whoever wanted to join would, and whoever didn't, well . . .

So, you'll understand when I tell you that one of my proudest moments was when my mother admitted that my brisket was better than hers. Holidays are different now—different foods and different traditions because of Leo. And the holidays don't suck anymore!

THREE-HOUR BRISKET

Growing up, the fundamental ingredient in everyone's brisket was Lipton's onion soup mix. Once we changed our diet, that would no longer work. My mother couldn't imagine making brisket without onion soup mix. She was stumped. So, I told her not to worry—*I* would make the brisket. Then came one of my proudest moments . . .

As my mother tasted my brisket, I waited patiently in anticipation of her approval. She isn't generous with compliments, especially when it comes to cooking. There's a lot of "That's not how I do it," whenever she is in my kitchen. To my astonishment, my mother could not stop raving about my brisket and how flavorful it was. The kids love it too, but who cares as long as my mother approves!

The Goods

- ♥ 3 organic garlic cloves, crushed
- ♥ 4–6 lb brisket
- ♥ 1½ tsp coarse kosher salt
- ♥ 1 tsp Jane's Krazy Mixed-Up Salt (my secret ingredient)
- ♥ ½ tsp ground organic rainbow peppercorns
- ♥ 4 organic carrots
- ♥ 2 large organic onions
- ♥ 3 organic celery stalks
- ♥ ½ cup organic beef broth

Putting Everything Together

1. Rub the crushed garlic into the brisket evenly.

2. Cover the meat with the kosher salt, Jane's Krazy Mixed-Up Salt, and pepper, and rub everything in. You can do this the night before and let the brisket sit overnight in the rub. If you do, put it in a plastic bag and keep in the fridge overnight.

3. Preheat the oven to 325 degrees.

4. Chop the carrots, onions, and celery into large chunks and line them on the bottom of a large covered roasting pan.

5. Place the brisket on top of the vegetables. Then pour in the beef broth.

6. Cover and cook for 3 hours.

It's best to buy brisket at a market that caters to a Jewish population. In this case, you want fat on your meat since that's where a lot of the flavor comes from, so buy first cut brisket. Typically, a serving size is one pound per person, so buy them a little bigger if you want leftovers.

I was taught that no matter what size the brisket is or how you prepare it, it always cooks for three hours (as determined by my mother). This is the only dish I know of that has such a definitive cook time. When making brisket, I hear my mother's voice in my head, repeating, "It cooks for three hours . . . it cooks for three hours." So, don't open the roasting pan until three hours have passed!

AUNT JACKIE'S PINEAPPLE SPOON BREAD

(Now available gluten-free and casein-free)

This is by far Leo's favorite dish. He asks me to make pineapple spoon bread a few times a week. Leo knows this recipe by heart. Once, he wanted to make it but we didn't have any pineapple, so we used apples instead. That's the great thing about cooking—you can always scrape something together from whatever you have in your fridge or cabinet.

The Goods

- 8 slices gluten-free bread
- 4 organic free-range eggs (or substitute with 1 cup organic applesauce)
- 1 stick dairy-free, soy-free butter substitute, melted
- ½ cup organic sugar
- ½ tsp gluten-free organic vanilla extract
- 1 large can crushed organic pineapple
- 1 tbsp organic cinnamon

Putting Everything Together

1. Preheat the oven to 350 degrees.

2. Tear the bread into bite-sized pieces.

3. Beat the eggs, melted butter substitute, sugar, and vanilla together with a beater. Leo loves using the beater, but he still needs close supervision.

4. In a large mixing bowl, combine the bread pieces, pineapple, and egg-butter-sugar mixture well. Children can use their hands to mix the ingredients.

5. Transfer the mixture to a baking dish and sprinkle cinnamon on top.

6. Bake for 45 minutes.

Food Outside the Kitchen

Exposing your children to food outside the kitchen can be both valuable and a lot of fun. We like to watch cooking shows at our house. *Cupcake Wars* and *Diners, Drive-Ins and Dives* fill up our DVR!

Leo started watching cooking videos on YouTube at a very young age. That was part of how I knew he was interested in cooking. He also plays iPad games that have to do with preparing food.

Apple picking in the fall, berry picking in the summer—we do it all. If it has to do with food, my kids are interested. We pick apples to make applesauce or apple crisps. It's a healthy and educational process to go through the food sequence from beginning to end, from farm to table. We haven't planted our own garden yet, but that might be something to think about for the springtime!

APRICOT CHICKEN

The Goods

- ♥ 4–5 lb whole organic chicken, washed and dried
- ♥ ½ tsp sea salt
- ♥ 1 medium organic orange
- ♥ 2 jars organic apricot fruit spread (I like sugar-free spreads)

Putting Everything Together

1. Preheat the oven to 450 degrees.

2. Place the chicken on a rack and sprinkle sea salt over it.

3. Slice the orange in half and squeeze the juice over the chicken.

4. Rub the apricot jam all over the chicken. Let the kids use their hands; it will be nice and sticky. Again, remember to have them wash their hands before and afterward.

5. Cook at 450 degrees for 15 minutes and reduce to 350 degrees, roasting the chicken for 20 minutes per pound. If the wings or legs start to get too crispy or dark, cover the tips with a bit of foil.

You can use any kind of jam or jelly you like. I choose to use an option that is lower in sugar as there is enough sweetness in this dish.

CRISPY GREEN BEAN CASSEROLE

The Goods

- ♥ 1½ cups gluten-free crispy fried onion topping (you can also buy allergy-safe versions at the store)

  1 large organic sweet onion, sliced thinly

  Organic chicken stock, to cover

  ¾ cup gluten-free all-purpose flour

  ¼ tsp fine organic sea salt

  Pinch of pepper

  1 tsp organic sugar

  Organic cooking oil, for the pan

- ♥ 1 lb organic green beans
- ♥ 2 tbsp organic olive oil
- ♥ 1 shallot, minced
- ♥ 2 garlic cloves, minced
- ♥ Organic sea salt, to taste
- ♥ Organic black pepper, to taste
- ♥ 1 cup organic mushrooms (button or baby portabella work well), finely chopped
- ♥ 2 tbsp organic all-purpose gluten-free flour (make sure it doesn't contain soy or nut flours)
- ♥ ¾ cup organic vegetable broth
- ♥ 1 cup organic unsweetened plain rice milk

Putting Everything Together: Gluten-Free Crispy Fried Onion Topping

1. Add the sliced onions into a mixing bowl and cover with chicken stock. Let this soak for a few minutes.

2. Mix together the flour, salt, pepper, and sugar.

3. Remove the onions from the stock. In batches, toss and cover onions with the flour mixture.

4. Heat cooking oil over medium-high heat in a large frying pan. In batches, gently put breaded onion slices into the oil and fry until golden brown. Flip them over halfway through.

5. Using a slotted spoon, remove fried onions from oil. Drain and cool on a paper towel and set aside.

Putting Everything Together: Crispy Green Bean Casserole

1. Preheat the oven to 400 degrees. Bring a large pot of water to a boil and salt well; it helps to season the green beans.

2. Wash the green beans. Remove tips and cut into halves.

3. Blanch the green beans by cooking in boiling water for 5 minutes. Drain them and place in ice water to stop them from cooking. Drain and set aside in a casserole dish.

4. Heat oil over medium heat in a large skillet and add shallot and garlic. Season with salt and pepper and stir. Cook for 2 to 3 minutes.

5. Add the mushrooms. Season with a little more salt and pepper. Cook about 3 to 4 minutes more or until lightly browned.

6. Sprinkle in flour and whisk to stir and coat the vegetables. Cook for about a minute. Then, slowly whisk in vegetable stock.

7. Add the rice milk and whisk again. Season with a little more salt and pepper and bring to a simmer. Simmer for 5 to 7 minutes more, until thick and bubbly.

8. Remove from heat and stir into the green beans. Add ½ cup of the gluten-free crispy fried onions into the mixture. Toss and stir until the green beans are thoroughly covered. Though it may look mushy, the green beans should stay firm. Top with the remaining fried onions.

9. Bake in the oven for 15 minutes, or until bubbly and slightly browned on top.

Try this recipe for a holiday meal and see if anyone notices that it's gluten- and dairy-free. Traditionally, most people use cream of mushroom soup for this dish. Here, we use natural mushrooms and eliminate all that unnecessary salt in canned soup.

GLAZED HONEY SWEETS

The Goods

- ♥ 1 large bag organic sweet potatoes or yams, cubed
- ♥ 2 medium butternut squashes, cubed
- ♥ 2 tbsp organic cooking oil
- ♥ ¼ cup organic light brown sugar
- ♥ 2 tsp organic cinnamon
- ♥ 2 tbsp organic honey

> Around Thanksgiving time, Trader Joe's sells large bags of sweet potatoes and butternut squash that are already cubed. I highly recommend "cheating" and buying them pre-cut because cubing vegetables is not a job for children.

Putting Everything Together

1. Preheat the oven to 375 degrees.

2. Put cubed sweet potatoes and squash in a baking dish. Drizzle oil evenly over the vegetables.

3. Sprinkle brown sugar and cinnamon over the vegetables. Be generous with the sugar and spread until the cubes are covered.

4. In a zigzag line, drizzle honey across the top. Give a little mix and drizzle one more round of honey.

5. Roast in the oven for about 40 minutes, mixing around once or twice. A nice cinnamon sugar glaze should form over the top.

> This dish is a great substitute for a traditional sweet potato casserole. You can add mini organic gluten-free marshmallows on top, if you like.

Cheating

For many years, we didn't eat out at restaurants at the beginning of our food journey. I was afraid, and I didn't trust that the ingredients were safe. Now, there are so many options for food allergy sufferers to eat out. Most restaurants have gluten-free items and some menus are even sensitive to food allergies. Be sure to tell your server about your child's allergies even if you are ordering something from the allergy-free menu.

I do allow Leo to eat regular chicken fingers on occasion if there is not much else for him to eat on the menu; just don't tell the TACA moms! Whenever we are out to eat with other children and they choose chicken fingers, I'll let Leo get them too. I use enzymes in these cases, but don't make it a habit. If your child does not have celiac disease or a true or severe allergy to gluten, lighten up once in a while. It will make your life easier and your child will feel happy and included. I may have to deal with strange behaviors over the next few days, but it subsides much quicker than it used to. I would not recommend doing this all of the time; that will cause problems.

I order fries for Leo at restaurants without obsessing over whether or not gluten items are cooked in the same oil. Burgers without buns are another easy restaurant item you can order.

Chinese food was a Sunday night ritual at my house before the food revolution, and it still is today. I have a local Chinese place that I trust. They know about Leo's allergies, they do not use MSG or additives, and they deliver! Leo usually gets spare ribs, fried rice, and sometimes chicken and broccoli. Chinese restaurants typically do use nuts and additives like MSG, so make sure you choose a place you know well. Build a relationship with your local spots so they will take special care to make sure your food is extra safe.

Other favorite places where we can get allergen-free eats are the Cheesecake Factory, Iron Hill Brewery, Jules Thin Crust, Bryn and Danes, Chipotle, Grub Burger, Zoe's Kitchen, and, my most favorite of them all, Sweet Freedom Bakery in Philadelphia. As much as we love to cook, we can't do it all of the time. It's refreshing to eat out once in a while.

BE THANKFUL FOR GLUTEN-FREE STUFFING

The Goods

- ♥ 3 tbsp organic high-heat cooking oil
- ♥ 2 organic medium onions, chopped
- ♥ 3 organic celery stalks, chopped
- ♥ 1 loaf of your favorite gluten free white bread
- ♥ 1 tsp organic sea salt
- ♥ 4 cracks/twists organic cracked black pepper
- ♥ 1 tsp fresh organic sage
- ♥ 1 tsp dried organic thyme, chopped
- ♥ 2 organic free-range eggs, beaten
- ♥ 2 cups organic chicken stock (homemade or store-bought gluten-free stock is fine)
- ♥ Vegan soy-free butter, for the baking dish

Putting Everything Together

1. Preheat your oven to 325 degrees.

2. Over medium heat, heat oil in a frying pan. Sauté the chopped onions and celery until golden brown. Remove and set aside.

3. Cut the bread with scissors into ¾-inch pieces and place in a large mixing bowl. Add the onions, celery, and spices into the bread mix.

4. Add the eggs to the mixture, along with the chicken stock. Mix thoroughly with your hands. Everyone should get their hands in there to "bless" the stuffing.

5. Grease a glass baking dish on all sides with butter. If you have butter in sticks, let your child rub it directly onto the baking dish. Spoon the mixture into the baking dish.

6. Bake for about 30 to 40 minutes or until the top is slightly brown and crispy.

Add any other ingredients you like to make this stuffing your own, such as carrots, sausage, or mushrooms—whatever makes it feel traditional for you.

HOLY PINEAPPLE GLAZED HAM

The Goods

- ♥ 6 ham steaks
- ♥ Dressing
  - 1 cup fresh pressed organic pineapple juice
  - 1 cup organic dark brown sugar
  - 4–6 fresh organic pineapple rings

Putting Everything Together

1. Preheat the oven to 350 degrees.

2. Place the ham in a roasting dish and dress it with pineapple juice and brown sugar.

3. Place pineapple rings around the ham in the bottom of the pan.

4. Heat in the oven for about 20 minutes or until the ham is warm. The ham is precooked, so you don't have to worry about cooking it; you just want to get a nice glaze and impart some flavor.

5. Slice the ham and remove the casing. Serve with the pineapple on top or to the side.

Depending on how many people you are serving, you can use half a ham or a whole boneless ham. It is important to buy a quality brand of ham that is free of allergens. Wellshire Farms makes allergen-free hams and they donate their money to a local autism school in my area.

Crispy Green Bean Casserole (see recipe on p. 173) goes nicely with this dish.

AUNT SHELL'S SWEET-AND-SOUR BALLS

Aunt Shell is a great cook! Michelle is not *really* the children's biological aunt; she's just one of those friends you are so close with that it feels like family. She is my sister from another mister, and my kids call her Aunt Shell. She is a much better cook than me and has spent many afternoons showing me how to make some of her dishes.

Aunt Shell cooks healthy and clean meals, and she always has a refrigerator full of fresh organic fruits, veggies, and snacks. Her sons Flynn and Charlie are great eaters; however, Flynn has a very serious peanut allergy. In Aunt Shell's kitchen, Flynn and Leo need not worry because Aunt Shell's house is also peanut-free!

The Goods

- ♥ 2½ lb organic meat mix, ground (You can mix beef, pork, lamb, etc. I like to buy from a market that caters to Jewish clientele.)
- ♥ 2 free-range organic eggs
- ♥ ½ cup EZ Gluten-Free Breadcrumbs (see recipe on p. 106)
- ♥ 2 cans organic whole cranberries
- ♥ 2 cans organic tomato sauce
- ♥ ¼ cup organic brown sugar
- ♥ 4 gluten-free ginger snaps (I added this ingredient from my mother's recipe)
- ♥ 6–8 fresh organic figs (optional; I added this ingredient as well)

Putting Everything Together

1. Put your ground meat in a large mixing bowl.

2. Beat eggs slightly in a separate bowl and mix in breadcrumbs.

3. Pour the breadcrumb mixture into the meat and mix thoroughly by hand. My kids love to smoosh their hands right in.

4. In a large sauce pot, heat cranberries, tomato sauce, and brown sugar together over medium-low heat until it comes to a slight boil.

5. Roll the meat mixture into small meatballs about the size of a Super Ball and drop them into the tomato-cranberry mix.

6. Crush the gluten-free ginger snaps. I put them in a baggie and let Leo bang on them with a wooden spoon until crushed.

7. Add in the crushed ginger snaps and whole figs.

8. Turn the heat down and simmer uncovered for about an hour.

PASS THE LATKES

Latkes are Jewish pancakes. They are delicious with applesauce! You can make your own applesauce by coring, peeling, and cooking apples, then blending them in your food processor.

If you don't want to fry the latkes, you can bake them in the oven instead.

The Goods

- ♥ 6 organic russet potatoes
- ♥ 1 organic onion
- ♥ ½ cup gluten-free flour mix
- ♥ 2 organic free-range eggs, beaten
- ♥ ½ teaspoon organic sea salt
- ♥ Organic high-heat cooking oil, for frying

Hanukkah

Putting Everything Together

1. Peel and grate potatoes into a deep bowl. Squeeze out some of the liquid by pressing down on the grated potatoes with your hands and removing excess liquid.

2. Peel and grate the onion and mix in with the potatoes.

3. Sift flour into the beaten eggs and add the salt.

4. Combine the potatoes and onion with the flour and egg mixture. Mix together using your hands.

5. Heat oil in a large frying pan. Drop spoonfuls of potato batter into the pan and fry until the edges are crispy. Flip and fry on the other side. Add more oil if needed.

6. Remove from the pan as soon as the latkes are browned. Place on paper towels to drain excess oil.

7. Serve hot with your favorite topping, such as applesauce.

SAFE SWEETS

"Sugar-Free"

The term "sugar-free" doesn't mean healthier. In fact, chemical sweeteners are poisonous to your health. Yes, sugar can be the enemy, but I'd take a small amount of real organic sugar any day over a low-calorie chemical sweetener. "Gluten-free" doesn't mean healthier either; in fact, pre-made GF snacks are often loaded with sugar.

We avoid common allergens such as gluten, casein, soy, and nuts because we may be very allergic or because they just don't agree with our bodies.

My seventy-year-old father, who is very health conscious, is constantly counting *calories*. What's with that business? He also thinks olive oil is the cure to anything. I don't get it. Eat healthy foods, eat when you're hungry, eat to live, don't live to eat—and it's all good, right?

If we stop thinking in terms of foods that are "free" in harmful things and start thinking inversely about what is naturally good to put in our bodies, then we can free ourselves from the prisons of counting calories and scrutinizing labels. It's actually very simple: whole foods, foods that contain very few ingredients, are just better for us.

YOUTUBE GUMMIES

If you have a child with autism, you might spend a lot of time listening to the hum of strange YouTube videos in the background like I do. Leo found these YouTube videos where people make tiny gummy candies in all kinds of different shapes. Leo's favorite is the dolphin gummy candy. To my surprise, I found out that a friend's child, who is not autistic, also enjoys watching these gummy-making videos. She found similar gummy-making trays on Amazon, and I was able to take Leo's YouTube obsession and turn it into a real-life cooking activity! A little less time on YouTube and something sweet and fun for us to do together is a great plan.

The Goods

♥ 1½ cups fresh pressed organic juice: You can make this in your juicer or buy freshly pressed juice at the store. Keep in mind that this will determine the flavor and color of your gummies.
  • Blueberries, blackberries, concord grapes: blue/purple gummies
  • Spinach, green grapes, cucumber, kale: green gummies
  • Peaches, mangoes, oranges, carrots: orange gummies
  • Strawberries, raspberries, red plums: red gummies
  • Avoid using the juice from pineapple and green apples as they don't set well

♥ 4 tbsp high-quality plain gelatin (try the brand Great Lakes or Agar Powder for a vegan version; quality is important to the outcome)

♥ 2–4 tbsp raw organic honey. (If you're using green or vegetable juices, use more honey; if you're using a sweeter juice, use less)

- ♥ Organic vanilla extract (optional; you can add other sweeteners besides honey if you like)
- ♥ Silicone gummy molds: Order a few different shapes and sizes from Amazon. This is a great birthday gift for other children on similar diets. You can also use ice cube trays.

You can always add ingredients like cod liver oil, elderberry, or probiotics to give your gummies a healthy boost. You may want to add a little more honey if you're doing this to hide the other flavors.

Putting Everything Together

1. In a medium saucepan over low heat, warm up your juice.

2. Sprinkle in the gelatin, slowly raising the heat to medium, mixing until the gelatin is completely dissolved. Don't let the mixture boil.

3. Add in the honey and vanilla extract. Gently stir until thoroughly dissolved (taste the liquid and adjust for desired sweetness).

4. Remove from stove and pour the mixture into your child's choice of gummy trays or ice cube trays. Be careful: the mixture is hot. I like to transfer it into a large measuring cup so I can pour it out of the spout—less mess.

5. Put in the fridge for 2 to 3 hours. Remove the candy gently from the trays. Of course, eat a few while you're doing this!

6. Store your gummies in an airtight container; they will last a bit longer if you store them in the fridge.

You can have a lot of fun making gummies in different colors, shapes, and sizes. We make bears, robots, and, of course, dolphins for Leo. This is a great way to get language out of a child and practice naming colors, animals, and shapes while you cook!

MERINGUE DROPS

The Goods

- ♥ 3 large egg whites from organic free-range eggs
- ♥ 1½ tsp organic vanilla extract
- ♥ ¼ tsp cream of tartar
- ♥ Pinch of sea salt
- ♥ ⅔ cup organic sugar

Putting Everything Together

1. Let the egg whites sit out in a bowl for 30 minutes at room temperature. Make sure all the yolk has been removed or the meringue will not work. Leo is great at separating the yolks from the whites!

2. Preheat the oven to 250 degrees. Line a baking sheet with parchment paper.

3. Using an electric hand mixer, beat in the vanilla, cream of tartar, and salt. Beat on medium until the mixture becomes foamy.

4. Gradually add in the sugar one tablespoon at a time. Beat the mixture on high speed in between each spoonful.

5. Continue beating until you get stiff glossy peaks, about 7 minutes.

6. Transfer mixture into a squeeze bottle with a large open tip, or use a plastic or pastry bag with a cut slit at the end.

7. Squeeze out one-inch dollops onto the baking sheet, leaving about 2 inches of space in between.

8. Bake for 45 minutes or until the meringue is firm.

9. Turn the oven off and leave the meringues in the oven for an hour. Do not open the oven. Finally, remove and let cool.

It's always nice to expose the kids to different textures when you're cooking—meringues have a very unique feel. They are seriously sugary, so save them for the most special of occasions.

ME LOVE COOKIES

Makes 24 cookies

Okay, everyone loves Cookie Monster from *Sesame Street*, right? Try adding some fun to cookie making with the kids by talking in a cookie monster voice or getting out a cookie monster doll and having him help make, or steal, the cookies. I know, I know, it's silly— but silly is good and fun!

The Goods

- 2½ cups gluten-free flour blend (Namaste Foods makes one that's dairy-, egg-, soy-, and nut-free)
- 1 tsp organic aluminum-free baking powder
- ½ tsp organic sea salt
- 1 cup organic sugar
- ¾ cup organic vegetable shortening, softened (not melted)
- 2 organic free-range eggs (or substitute ½ cup organic applesauce or 2 bananas)
- 2 tsp organic vanilla extract
- Chocolate chips (optional)
- Cinnamon or sugar, to sprinkle (optional)

Putting Everything Together

1. Mix flour, baking powder, and salt in a bowl just for the dry ingredients.

2. In a separate large mixing bowl, beat the sugar into softened shortening until smooth.

3. Add in eggs (or applesauce, or banana) and vanilla. Beat until smooth.

4. Slowly pour in the dry flour and baking powder mix.

5. Add in chocolate chips if you're using them. The kids can mix them in with their hands.

6. Let the cookie mix stand in the refrigerator for about 20 to 30 minutes. This is really hard with children who have little patience, so let them do something fun in the meantime to take their minds off the cookies. Have them go outside or into another room.

7. Preheat your oven to 375 degrees. Line your baking sheet with parchment paper.

8. Scoop chilled dough onto a baking sheet with an ice cream scooper. This is a great trick and a good opportunity for fine motor practice for kids who need it. Don't fill a whole scoop or your cookies will be too big. Make them about a half-inch thick and leave enough space in between the scoops because these cookies spread quite a bit during cooking.

9. Feel free to sprinkle a little cinnamon or sugar on top of your cookies, but not if you added chocolate chips. That is just too much going on!

10. Bake for 8 to 10 minutes in the oven or until the edges are browned.

You can add in dairy-free chocolate chips if your child likes that; Leo doesn't!

Birthdays

Leo was affectionately known as "Spike" until he was born. I intensely recall the feelings that came over me the day I took a positive pregnancy test—joy, excitement, and *terror*! I was terrified that it was actually positive. I wasn't expecting a baby to happen that fast! I was barely able to take care of myself, let alone another human being!

Nine months later, Leo Thomas Vernacchio was born, weighing seven pounds and three ounces with a full head of hair. Leo was a typical baby and met all of his milestones for the first twenty months of his life. He did have problems with reflux and feeding, however. Pediatricians are not quick to put babies on prescription formulas, so we tried soy-based formulas, pre-digested formulas, etc., but nothing seemed to work. Eventually, I learned that Leo was actually allergic to milk. When I tried giving him milk for the first time, he spit it up immediately. It was certainly not helpful that Leo had been drinking formula that he was allergic to for the entire first year of his life. Between nine and twelve months, Leo tried different foods. He would occasionally have puffy eyes or a mystery rash.

Leo celebrated a traditional first birthday party with a table full of twenty-five children eating chicken fingers and birthday cake.

In 2006, Leo regressed very quickly over the holidays. He went from a happy, engaged little boy who would sit in his highchair, giggling and playing silly games with me, to a sad, withdrawn child who stared out the window, cried all the time, and no longer responded to his

name. One afternoon, I was trying to console him by rocking and bopping in a certain pattern that had begun to settle him more recently. Leo tapped on my shoulder in a repetitive pattern that he had never done before, like when someone taps their fingers on a table in an impatient manner. Right there it hit me—*autism*.

I knew nothing about autism other than having seen *Rain Man*, which I just recently watched again after not having seen it in twenty years. Although the character Raymond is very high functioning in the film, his set-offs, meltdowns, speech patterns, mannerisms, and reactions to unpleasant sensory experiences are portrayed by Dustin Hoffman in an authentic way that is comparable to how Leo sometimes responds to the world.

What does this story have to do with birthdays and cakes, you ask? Well, Leo's birthday is very bittersweet for me, more bitter than sweet. Truth be told, it makes me very depressed. First, his food allergies pose a huge problem for preparing party food and ordering any kind of cool character cakes. Secondly, until about a few years ago, Leo didn't seem to care about his birthday celebrations, or even realize it was his birthday, for that matter. Birthday parties are loud and over-the-top, with a lot of sensory stimulation. Presents are also stressful. I spent years buying Leo toys that he *never* played with.

The real heartbreaker is that as Leo gets older every year, I see a larger gap between him and his peers. He gets bigger and further from the cute toddler who doesn't seem too different from the other kids. Another year goes by where he hasn't learned to read, add, and subtract, and the stimmy behaviors and weird noises I hoped he would outgrow are still there. Each year Leo gets older is another year closer to adulthood for him. I all but have to mentally block out the thought of what will happen to Leo when I die. Where will he live? Who will take care of him? Will someone hurt him? These are incredibly difficult thoughts, but more difficult is the possible reality of those thoughts.

On Leo's birthday every year, I am reminded of the loss of all the hopes and dreams I had for my firstborn child, dreams of us taking family vacations, attending sporting events, going to restaurants, or celebrating holidays and traditions. There is an intense sadness and grief that accompanies this thought. Everything is different because Leo has autism. Each year he turns older, I feel like I'm losing him more.

"EVERY CLASS HAS A KID WITH FOOD ALLERGIES" BIRTHDAY CUPCAKES

I feel compelled to be honest here: I'm no Betty Crocker; I don't like baking. It's hard. My mother never baked and, therefore, never taught me. Aunt Jackie is the baker of the family; it calms her nerves, or so she says. Well, baking does the opposite for me and always makes a big mess. Baking is more of a science and I have to make sure the chemistry actually works. I am not embarrassed to use store-bought cake mixes and icings; just don't tell the other moms.

Cherrybrook Kitchen makes fabulous gluten-, dairy-, egg-, and peanut-free products. They also sell chocolate and vanilla frosting mixes that are premade. Remember—it's okay to cheat sometimes. I always keep some in my cupboard in case I need cupcakes in a pinch. I also freeze any leftover cupcakes and send some into school so there is a special treat on hand for Leo if there is a birthday or a celebration.

Even in my daughter's school, you are no longer able to send anything that has a potential allergen, especially peanut. In 2013, it was reported that 1 in 13 children has a food allergy and that food allergies increased 50 percent between 1997 and 2011. So, I say, why bother making something that is *not* allergy-free? Send allergy-free cupcakes for school parties along with a printout of the ingredients. This way no child in the class will feel left out.

The Goods: Cupcake

- ♥ Store-bought gluten-, dairy-, egg-, and nut-free vanilla cupcake mix
- ♥ ½ cup organic vegetable shortening, melted (Spectrum makes a great organic non-GMO butter-flavored vegetable shortening)
- ♥ 1 tbsp aluminum-free baking powder
- ♥ ½ tsp organic vanilla extract
- ♥ 1 organic banana (makes cupcakes moist and adds flavor)

When choosing vanilla extract, make sure it doesn't contain alcohol because that may contain gluten. Organic vanilla extract is usually safe.

Putting Everything Together: Cupcake

1. Preheat the oven according to the instructions on the box of the cupcake mix.

2. Add cake mix, melted shortening, baking powder, vanilla, and filtered water (if called for) into a large mixing bowl.

3. Briefly beat with an electric hand beater until smooth.

4. Add the banana last and continue beating until smooth. I let Leo do this part, though he still needs very close supervision. I leave the beater unplugged until we are absolutely ready to use it. If not, he will be beating without me the minute I turn around to get something. I worry that he might put his fingers in the bowl while the beater is on.

5. Let the mix sit for a few minutes while you line the cupcake tray with decorative cupcake wrappers.

6. Transfer the cake mix to a measuring cup or squeeze bottle. Let your child squeeze the mix into the cupcake pan. The squeeze bottle should slow down the pouring and prevent too much from going into one cup.

7. Bake the cupcakes for the amount of time stated on the box instructions. You can add an extra minute or two for the additional banana.

I don't think parents of children without food allergies make cupcakes from scratch either. They are likely using mixes from a box too.

You may allow your child to lick the beaters, but only when you are done. It is important to teach your child not to lick or taste too much while cooking, especially if they might want to work in food service one day. This will be a challenge!

While your cupcakes cool, choose to prepare either chocolate or white frosting:

The Goods: Chocolate Frosting

♥ ¼ cup or ½ stick dairy- and soy-free buttery spread or shortening, softened (not melted)
♥ 2 cups organic powdered sugar
♥ ¼ cup vanilla rice milk
♥ ¾ cup unsweetened pure cocoa powder
♥ ½ tsp organic vanilla extract

The Goods: White Frosting

♥ 6 tbsp dairy- and soy-free buttery spread or shortening, softened (not melted)
♥ 1¾ cups organic powdered sugar
♥ 2 tsp organic apple cider vinegar
♥ 1 tsp organic vanilla extract

Putting Everything Together: Frosting

1. With an electric hand beater, beat the shortening into the powdered sugar on low speed, otherwise the powdered sugar will fly all over the place.

2. Once you get that smooth texture, add in the remaining ingredients from either the chocolate or white frosting recipes and beat on high speed until the frosting has a stiff consistency.

3. Again, using a squeeze bottle or plastic bag with the tip cut off, swirl the frosting onto the cupcakes, starting from the outside and spiraling into the center until you get a nice point in the middle.

You can decorate your cupcakes with homemade gummies, gluten-free sprinkles, or decorative toothpicks!

PEACE OF MIND POPS

You want your child to feel included when the rest of the kids in the neighborhood are running toward the music of the ice cream man or enjoying a sweet frozen treat at summer camp. Typical ice pops, though cold and refreshing, are like little frozen sugar sticks made from artificial flavors and dye. This recipe is easy—and totally healthy.

The Goods

♥ Ice pop trays, ice cube trays, or clear plastic cups (Buying actual popsicle molds will allow the ice pop sticks to stay nicely in place)

♥ Freshly diced fruit: kiwis, strawberries, whole blueberries, peaches (This is optional; you can stick with only juice if your child doesn't want fruit in their ice pops)

♥ Organic fresh pressed juice, whatever flavor or color your child likes (You can use a juicer or buy freshly pressed juices at the store. You may want to cut the juice with some water to reduce the sweetness.)

Putting Everything Together

1. Fill the popsicle molds about halfway with small pieces of fruit. Keep them looking pretty.

2. Pour the juice into the molds, filling them to the top.

3. Place in the freezer until frozen. Remove the pops. If you have leftover juice and fruits, refill the mold so you will have a full stash of ice pops all summer.

If your child goes to summer camp, talk to the camp counselors and bring enough popsicles to leave in the camp's freezer for the whole summer. You can also explore the option of coming in and making popsicles onsite with the whole bunk for a fun activity. I love to go to Leo's school or camp and carry out food and cooking activities. Children love it, and since you are an allergy-free momma, the other parents need not worry, especially with this basic fruit-only recipe for popsicles!

CHOCOLATE LOVE

On special occasions we break out the chocolate fountain that Grandma bought the kids. Fun and messy fondue! It's also a good time to put *Willy Wonka and the Chocolate Factory* on to get the children in the mood. After this dessert, the grownups can sit and talk over coffee while the kids veg out on the couch with full bellies, watching one of the most classic movies of all time. Only the original for my kids. I love Johnny Depp; however, he does give off a bit of a creepy vibe in the Tim Burton remake. Scarlett agrees!

The Goods

- ♥ Organic high-heat cooking oil, for the pan
- ♥ 2 cups dairy-free chocolate chips (I like the brand Enjoy Life; their chips come in different sizes)
- ♥ Organic strawberries
- ♥ Organic bananas
- ♥ Organic gluten-free marshmallows

Putting Everything Together

1. Drop some organic oil into a medium saucepan to keep it oiled.

2. Melt chocolate chips in the saucepan over medium heat. Transfer melted chocolate to the fountain.

3. Using wooden skewers, dip strawberries, bananas, marshmallows, or whatever goodies you love into the chocolate.

SWEET AND SALTY BANANAS

The Goods

♥ ½ cup dairy-free chocolate chips (I like the brand Enjoy Life; their chips come in different sizes)

♥ 2 organic bananas, cut into chunks

♥ ½ tsp coarse sea salt

♥ Organic powdered sugar

Putting Everything Together

1. Melt the chocolate over medium heat in a medium pot.

2. Add the bananas to the chocolate. Mix in ½ tsp of sea salt.

3. Carefully pour the banana-chocolate mixture onto a large plate. Sprinkle powdered sugar on top.

Chocolate contains phenols, which may affect some children with food sensitivities. You may want to consider using an enzyme that breaks down phenols before letting your child eat. Houston Enzymes makes a good one.

ICE CREAM OF CHAMPIONS

You can make fruit-only ice cream out of pretty much any fruit you choose with a Champion Juicer. Freeze bananas, strawberries, melons, coconuts, or any other fruit, really, and put through the juicer to create an icy, smooth, soft serve–textured dessert. I always keep bananas in my freezer for ice cream and smoothies. If your bananas are turning brown, peel and freeze them. You will be happy you did that when you're next craving a smoothie or frozen dessert. These types of juicers can be very pricey, but they are a good investment in healthy eating.

How It All Happened

Whenever I asked my mother for a recipe, I would always get the same response: "You know I never measure." I would remember parts of her recipes from watching her cook and then call her every five minutes while I was cooking to get guidance. I began to replace my mom's ingredients with organic, gluten-free, dairy-free, soy-free, and nut-free ingredients. The staple dishes that I grew up on began to morph into healthier and allergy-free dishes. Now Leo, Scarlett, and I cook these family dishes together. We hope your family enjoys them too!

"Be the change you wish to see in the world." —Gandhi

"Don't compare yourself to other mothers. We are all losing our shit, some of us just hide it better than others." —Anonymous Facebook Mom

"Autism is different, and different can be beautiful." —Erica Daniels

Karma (Thanks)

> Karma has no menu. You get served what you deserve.

You are the great love of my life, Leo Thomas Vernacchio.

Raising you is a beautiful and painstaking journey of love. Letting go of *my* hopes and dreams for you is undeniably hard. My heart will always be a bit broken. Yet, I am eternally grateful for *you* and for the gifts you have blessed upon my heart, my life, and my soul. You give me purpose and passion, perspective and hope. You are my perfectly imperfect gift. My heart aches for my son to know the meaning of these words.

Allergen-Free Family Cookbook was a true labor of love. Cooking with my children, sharing what we do every day, and having the opportunity to inspire others is more than I could have ever dreamed. To have a life bursting with purpose and passion is to have a full and beautiful life.

A shout-out to the laptop my parents gifted me and to my over-ear Beats for being my only "office" in a very busy life. Thank you to Dave Matthews Band and Ed Sheeran for mostly being the soundtrack while I wrote this book. Thank you for T-Swift radio dance parties with my kids in our kitchen. Thank you to tequila on the rough nights and the hot yoga mornings to cleanse afterward. Thank you to life for knocking me down so many times and never giving me any choice but to get up.

Props to the *best* pep talk I've ever received exactly when I needed it most. David Goldstein, you have mad skills and something perfectly clicked during your hysterical rant about Broadway and other things. Thank you for reminding me of *who the ^@#* I am*! You are the proof that people come into our lives for a reason. Thank you.

Thank you to my editor, Kim Lim, for putting up with my first-time author syndrome!

Thank you to Ed Cunicelli for dedicating yourself and your time to the task of snapping some great photos of my child who never keeps still!

Gratitude for these Warrior Fathers:

Ken Siri—for sharing your inspirational story in *Big Daddy Autism* and inspiring me to do something Bigger, also. Thank you for being the kind of person who does things for others who could never repay you. It is because of you that *Allergen-Free Family Cookbook* is realized and published.

Louis Conte—for your unwavering commitment to my family. Thank you for the tireless advocacy work you do for all of our children.

Tony Lyons—for generously giving us this opportunity that we may never have received elsewhere. Thank you for realizing my dream of creating this book together, with and for Leo. Leo thanks you for supporting his accomplishment and giving him something to be proud of. Thank you for your commitment to publishing books about autism and by autism families.

To the people I have the privilege of calling family:

I feel lucky to have a mother and father who raised me to feel empathy, to be kind to others, and to always be generous to those who are less fortunate. Thank you, Mom and Dad, for inviting those who didn't have a place to go for dinner to *our* home, where they could sit around our table. Now *my* table too, no matter how big or small, will always have a place for those who wish to share it.

Leo's therapists, many whom have come and gone over the years—you are a light when it is dark, a support when we need it, and a part of our family forever.

Thank you, Michelle, for sharing recipes, for your rock star–style, and for your laughter. You have a kind spirit and a generous soul. You are my sister from another mother, and you are another mother to my daughter. Most of all, thank you for helping me get my groove back.

Cousin Vikki—thank you for taking a special interest in Leo and in me. Thank you for generously giving us your time, skills, and resources for our cause. I am proud to be your family any which way we look at it.

To my fellow warrior mothers, I can feel your inspirations from around the globe. Your dedication to your children, to the causes, and to one another is unparalleled.

I am you. You are me. We are family. Never give up.

Erica Daniels is an author, autism advocate, healthy cook, music lover, and single mother of Leo who struggles with autism and chronic health issues. Erica's life changed and gained new purpose after her son was diagnosed with autism in 2007. Specific dietary interventions and natural medications help ease Leo's debilitating anxiety and OCD and have improved the quality of life for Leo's entire family. If you'd like to learn more about medical cannabis for autism, please visit hopegrowsforautism.org.

CONVERSION CHARTS

METRIC AND IMPERIAL CONVERSIONS

(These conversions are rounded for convenience)

Ingredient	Cups/Tablespoons/ Teaspoons	Ounces	Grams/Milliliters
Butter	1 cup = 16 tablespoons = 2 sticks	8 ounces	230 grams
Cheese, shredded	1 cup	4 ounces	110 grams
Cream cheese	1 tablespoon	0.5 ounce	14.5 grams
Cornstarch	1 tablespoon	0.3 ounce	8 grams
Flour, all-purpose	1 cup/1 tablespoon	4.5 ounces/0.3 ounce	125 grams/8 grams
Flour, whole wheat	1 cup	4 ounces	120 grams
Fruit, dried	1 cup	4 ounces	120 grams
Fruits or veggies, chopped	1 cup	5 to 7 ounces	145 to 200 grams
Fruits or veggies, puréed	1 cup	8.5 ounces	245 grams
Honey, maple syrup, or corn syrup	1 tablespoon	0.75 ounce	20 grams
Liquids: cream, milk, water, or juice	1 cup	8 fluid ounces	240 milliliters
Oats	1 cup	5.5 ounces	150 grams
Salt	1 teaspoon	0.2 ounce	6 grams
Spices: cinnamon, cloves, ginger, or nutmeg (ground)	1 teaspoon	0.2 ounce	5 milliliters
Sugar, brown, firmly packed	1 cup	7 ounces	200 grams
Sugar, white	1 cup/1 tablespoon	7 ounces/0.5 ounce	200 grams/12.5 grams
Vanilla extract	1 teaspoon	0.2 ounce	4 grams

Fahrenheit	Celsius	Gas Mark
225°	110°	¼
250°	120°	½
275°	140°	1
300°	150°	2
325°	160°	3
350°	180°	4
375°	190°	5
400°	200°	6
425°	220°	7
450°	230°	8

INDEX